Of Thee I Sing

Of Thee I Sing

Lyrics and Music for America's Most Patriotic Songs

JERRY SILVERMAN

CITADEL PRESS
Kensington Publishing Corp.
www.kensingtonbooks.com

CITADEL PRESS BOOKS are published by
Kensington Publishing Corp.
850 Third Avenue
New York, NY 10022

All Kensington titles, imprints, and distributed lines are available at special quan-
tity discounts for bulk purchases for sales promotions, premiums, fund-raising,
educational, or institutional use. Special book excerpts or customized printings can
also be created to fit specific needs. For details, write or phone the office of the
Kensington special sales manager: Kensington Publishing Corp., 850 Third
Avenue, New York, NY 10022, attn: Special Sales Department,
phone 1-800-221-2647.

Citadel Press and the Citadel Logo are trademarks of Kensington Publishing Corp.

First printing: May 2002

10 9 8 7 6 5 4 3 2

Printed in the United States of America

Library of Congress Control Number: 2001099798

ISBN: 0-8065-2395-6

Contents

☆ ──────────────────────────────── ☆

v

The Civil War

World War One

World War Two

Americans All

Contents

Contents

Introduction

Our country was born in struggle, and as with all social upheavals, song played an integral part in its birth. When British tea was dumped into Boston Harbor, the splash it made found its musical echo in "Revolutionary Tea." "Yankee Doodle" transformed a mocking appellation of "upstart" Americans ("Stuck a feather in his cap . . .") into a rousing affirmation of American humor and determination.

As the years rolled on, each new test of our mettle inevitably inspired poets and composers to chronicle the events. The War of 1812 gave us the immortal "Star Spangled Banner" as well as the sprightly "Battle of New Orleans." Not all songs celebrate battles and victories. "Remember the Alamo" is a rallying cry; "Green Grow the Lilacs" is a tender love ballad sung by the troops in that same Mexican War. The national upheaval that was the Civil War produced an outpouring of song unequaled in our history. That terrible struggle, which cost us more than 600,000 American lives—Northern and Southern—left an incredibly rich musical legacy. Songs were written and sung by both sides on every aspect of the war. These songs include stirring marching songs ("The Battle Cry of Freedom"), sentimental ballads ("Tenting on the Old Camp Ground"), descriptions of battles ("Roll, *Alabama,* Roll"), and election campaign songs ("Lincoln and Liberty").

By the time we entered World War One, Tin Pan Alley was in full swing and its songwriters were more than equal to the task, penning tunes in a variety of styles—from rousing ("Over There") to syncopated ("We're Going to Celebrate the End of the War in Ragtime"). The songsmiths of World War Two continued the tradition of the popular song in the service of the country ("We Did It Before and We Can Do It Again"), as well as mining the rich repertoire of folk songs (" 'Round and Around Hitler's Grave," adapted from "Old Joe Clark").

Not all of our patriotic songs were composed in wartime. Patriotic sentiments flow naturally in our national conscience. "America the Beautiful" and "My Country 'Tis of Thee" have served us well in times of peace as well as war. "This Land Is Your Land" and

"We Shall Overcome" express our feelings in simple and direct terms. "The Stars and Stripes Forever" will forever set our feet to tapping.

Of Thee I Sing offers to the American people this unmatched wealth of unashamed patriotism in the most basic of all modes of expression: song. Keep the tradition alive by singing these songs loud and clear!

The Revolutionary War

Free America

Joseph Warren was one of the most prominent of the early revolutionary leaders, on a par with Samuel Adams and John Hancock. It was he who dispatched Paul Revere on his famous midnight ride. He became president of the Massachusetts Provincial Congress on April 23, 1775, and head of the committee to organize an army. It was no accident that he set his fiery revolutionary text to a well-known British tune, "The British Grenadiers." That was a surefire way to ensure that his composition would get sung. Popular poet-songwriters from Robert Burns to Woody Guthrie have always recognized the advantage of combining new words with old melodies. Warren's musical choice may have also been influenced by the fact that many prominent people in England were sympathetic to the American cause. Among them was Edward Gibbon, author of *The Decline and Fall of the Roman Empire,* who was at that time a member of Parliament. This would, perhaps, account for the literary references to Greek and Roman antiquity in the first verse.

The song appeared in colonial newspapers in 1774. Warren was later killed at the Battle of Bunker Hill on June 16, 1775, at the age of thirty-four.

According to the demands of rhyme, "America" is sometimes pronounced "Americay."

Free America

Words by Dr. Joseph Warren **Tune: "The British Grenadiers"**

G Bm Em D7 G D7 G Em C D7 G
That seat of sci-ence, Ath - ens, And earth's proud mis-tress, Rome; Where
G Bm Em D7 G D7 G Em C D7 G
now are all their glo - ries? We scarce can find a tomb. Then
G7 C G D7
guard your rights, A - mer - i - cans, Nor stoop to law - less sway, Op -

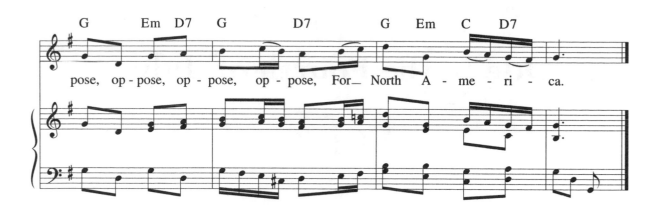

pose, op-pose, op-pose, op-pose, For— North A - me - ri - ca.

We led fair freedom hither,
And lo, the desert smiled!
A paradise of pleasure
Was opened in the wild!
Your harvest, bold Americans,
No power shall snatch away!
Huzza, huzza, huzza, huzza,
   For free America.

Torn from a world of tyrants,
Beneath the western sky,
We formed a new dominion,
A land of liberty.
The world shall own we're masters here,
Then hasten on the day:
Oppose, oppose, oppose, oppose
   For free America.

Lift up your hands, ye heroes,
And swear with proud disdain,
The wretch that would ensnare you,
Shall lay his snares in vain.
Should Europe empty all her force,
We'll meet her in array,
And fight and shout, and shout and fight
   For North America.

Some future day shall crown us
The masters of the main.
Our fleets shall speak in thunder
To England, France and Spain;
And the nations o'er the ocean spread
Shall tremble and obey
The sons, the sons, the sons, the sons
   Of brave America.

Ode to the Fourth of July

It is a fitting historical coincidence that "Ode to the Fourth of July" was composed in 1789, the year of the French Revolution. Horatio Garnett set Daniel George's flowery text to an appropriately majestic Handelian oratorical-style melody. British-influenced melodies, harmonies, and rhythms—not to mention poetical turns of phrase and image—were still very much in vogue in late-eighteenth-century America. It was not until later in our nation's cultural growth that poets and composers developed their own "American voices."

Ode to the Fourth of July

'Tis done, the e - dict past, by Heav - en de - creed,___ And Han - cock's___ name con - firms the glo - rious deed. On this au - spi - cious morn was___ In - de - pen - dence___

See haughty Britain sending hosts of foes,
With vengeance our freedom to oppose.
But Washington the great,
Dispelled impending fate,
And spurned each plan.
Americans combine to hail the godlike man. *Chorus*

Ode to the Fourth of July

9

Revolutionary Tea

When, in the 1770s, the Dutch East India Company began to sell its tea in the Colonies at lower prices than the British did, the ensuing crisis quickly developed to much more than a tempest in a teapot. The British East India Company, which heretofore had had a monopoly on tea sales in North America, saw its sales of tea drop off precipitously. Its warehouses started to fill up with unsold tea. Financial disaster loomed. The Americans were happy to drink Dutch tea instead of British; it all came from the same part of the world and tasted the same. And of course, now it was cheaper. The British had to do something about their losses—and something was done. In London, Parliament passed the Tea Act in 1773. A duty of three pence per pound was placed on all Dutch tea imported to America. The British could control this because the tea was transported on British ships. British tea could now compete in price with Dutch tea. The directors of the British East India Company were delighted; the Americans were outraged.

The Americans feared that if the British could set the price of tea, they could use their power to raise the prices of other products as well. They held antitax protests in New York, Philadelphia, and Boston. Their rallying cry was "No taxation without representation!"

When the first tea ships arrived in Boston Harbor in November 1773, people flocked together in mass meetings and demanded that the cargo be returned to England. But Governor Hutchinson, a loyal subject of King George III, insisted that the tea duties first be paid.

It was then that the people of Boston took matters into their own hands. A crowd gathered at the Old South Church on the evening of December 16. At a signal from Samuel Adams (whose cousin John would become the second president of the United States in 1796), a group of men disguised as Mohawks in Indian war paint rushed to the pier, boarded the ships, and dumped all 342 chests of tea overboard.

This bold deed was quickly dubbed the Boston Tea Party. Word of the Tea Party spread throughout the Colonies. In Charleston, South Carolina, a cargo of tea was seized for nonpayment of duties and was simply left to rot in a warehouse. In Annapolis, Maryland, a shipment was burned. In New York City, a group calling itself the Sons of Liberty held its own tea party.

The Parliament in London was furious about this open disobedience of British laws. Things were getting very tense between England and its North American colonies. War was definitely drawing near. The mocking words and sprightly tune of "Revolutionary Tea" served to keep the teakettle boiling.

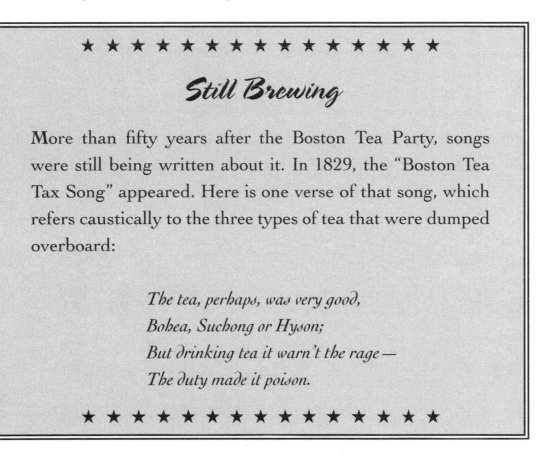

★ ★ ★ ★ ★ ★ ★ ★ ★ ★ ★ ★ ★ ★ ★ ★ ★

Still Brewing

More than fifty years after the Boston Tea Party, songs were still being written about it. In 1829, the "Boston Tea Tax Song" appeared. Here is one verse of that song, which refers caustically to the three types of tea that were dumped overboard:

> The tea, perhaps, was very good,
> Bohea, Suchong or Hyson;
> But drinking tea it warn't the rage —
> The duty made it poison.

★ ★ ★ ★ ★ ★ ★ ★ ★ ★ ★ ★ ★ ★ ★ ★ ★

Revolutionary Tea

ocean of water be - tween._____ The tea.

three pence a pound on the

Of three pence a pound on the tea._____

"Now mother, dear mother," the daughter replied,
"I shan't do the thing that you ax;
I'm willing to pay a fair price for the tea,
But never a three-penny tax."
"You shall," quoth the mother, and reddened with rage,
"For you're my own daughter, you see.
And sure 'tis quite proper the daughter should pay
Her mother a tax on the tea,
Her mother a tax on the tea."

And so the old lady her servant called up,
And packed off a budget of tea.
And eager for three pence a pound, she put in
Enough for a large family.
She ordered her servant to bring home the tax,
Declaring her child should obey,
Or old as she was, and a woman most grown,
She'd half whip her life away,
She'd half whip her life away.

The tea was conveyed to the daugher's front door,
All down by the ocean side,
But the bouncing girl poured out every pound
In the dark and the boiling tide.
And then she called out to the Island Queen,
"Oh mother, dear mother," quoth she,
"Your tea you may have when it is steeped enough,
But never a tax from me,
But never a tax from me."

Revolutionary Tea

Ballad of Bunker Hill

On the evening of June 16, 1775, about 800 American troops from Massachusetts and 200 from Connecticut, under the command of Colonel William Prescott, were sent out to fortify and occupy two high hills, Bunker and Breed's, near the north shore of Boston. They worked throughout the night to build a dirt fort on the top of Breed's Hill (which is now called Bunker Hill). At daybreak, they were discovered by the British, who began to fire at them from their men-o'-war in Boston Harbor as well as nearby cannons.

British General Gage sent a force of more than 2,300 troops under the command of Major General William Howe, with orders to attack the Americans and drive them from the hill. The patriots were outnumbered more than two to one. They were in a tight spot, and they knew it. There was no way that, behind the dirt wall of their fort, they could be resupplied with ammunition once the battle had begun. They could not waste their precious gunpowder and bullets by shooting wildly at the advancing British troops.

In a command that has been echoed down through the years, the Americans were ordered: "Don't fire until you see the whites of their eyes!"

Closer and closer came the British, advancing slowly and steadily up the hill in closed ranks. They peppered the defenders with shot and shell. When the first wave of Redcoats was practically at the fort, the order was given: *"Fire!"*

With a roar, the American guns opened up. Down went the leading ranks of the Redcoats. Caught by surprise, the remainder quickly retreated down the hill, only to regroup and attack once more. Once more they were driven back.

For a third time, the line of Redcoats marched up the hill. The patriots, many of whom were now out of ammunition, were forced to give up their positions and run for their lives. The British had won the day.

Or had they? British losses were extremely heavy. A staggering 1,054 men were either killed or wounded. The Americans suffered a loss of 450 men killed, captured, or wounded.

Both sides had paid a high price, but the British, in capturing the hill, had lost almost half their men—killed, captured, or wounded. They were so stunned by the fierce fighting of the young American army that they never took full advantage of their victory. They failed to fortify the area, and by March 1776, George Washington, who was by then in command of the American army, drove the British out of Boston for good.

Ballad of Bunker Hill

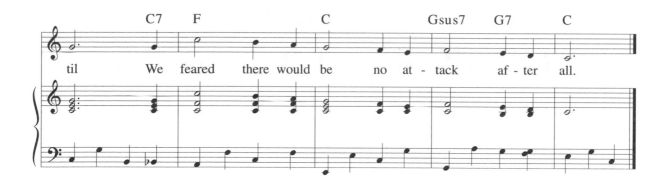

til   We feared   there would be   no at - tack   af - ter   all.

Let the foeman draw nigh till the white of his eye
Comes in range of your rifles, and then let it fly,
And show to Columbia, to Britain and fame,
How justice smiles awful when freemen take aim!

But when they got ready and all came along,
We were not a-feared and we welcomed 'em strong.
The way they marched up the hillside wasn't slow;
We held fire till the word and then laid the lads low.

But who shall declare the end of the affair,
At sundown there wasn't a man of us there.
We didn't depart till we'd given 'em some.
We used up our powder and had to go home!

The Riflemen of Bennington

In June 1777, British General John Burgoyne marched his troops down from Canada, heading for Albany, New York. He hoped to link up with troops under the command of General William Howe, who was supposed to advance northward along the Hudson River from New York City. The idea was to control the Hudson Valley, thereby cutting off New England from the rest of the colonies and increasing Great Britain's chances of winning the war.

The problem with this long-distance battle plan was that Burgoyne, at the northern end, had no way of communicating rapidly with Howe, at the southern end. On July 30, Burgoyne reached Fort Edward on the Hudson, about 45 miles north of Albany, but had a difficult time making his way through the deep, trackless woods. Meanwhile, unbeknownst to Burgoyne, Howe—instead of moving up the Hudson—set off to attack Philadelphia, the patriot capital.

At Fort Edward, Burgoyne was in a desperate situation. His men were running low on food and ammunition. Their supplies came from Montreal, Canada, which was a long way off. He had hoped that the local population would come to his aid, but the Americans remained true to the patriot cause. When he talked local Indians into fighting against the civilians, he angered the local population even more.

Burgoyne needed to do something quickly to take the pressure off his troops. On August 13, he sent a force of some 1,200 men to Bennington, Vermont—about 35 miles to the southeast—to capture supplies and terrorize the countryside. The commanding officer was the mercenary Hessian Colonel Friedrich Baum.

Baum was met by nearly 2,000 Green Mountain Boys, militiamen organized by Ethan Allen and under the command of General John Stark, from part of New Hampshire (now Vermont) and Massachusetts. "Johnny" Stark's Green Mountain Boys soundly defeated the enemy, killing 300 men and capturing more than 700. Baum himself died from his wounds. This American victory put an end to the British plan to control the Hudson Valley and cut off New England. It was a turning point in the war.

Although this encounter is called the Battle of Bennington, it was actually fought about 5 miles away, near the town of Hoosick, New York. The Bennington Battle Monument, a 301-foot shaft erected at the site, was at the time the tallest such monument in the world.

As for General Burgoyne, his fortunes declined after this debacle and ended with his defeat and surrender at the Battle of Saratoga the following October 17. His ill-advised campaign was summed up in this impudent quatrain:

> *In seventeen hundred and seventy-seven,*
> *General Burgoyne set out for Heaven;*
> *But as the Yankees would rebel,*
> *He missed his route and went to Hell.*

The Riflemen of Bennington

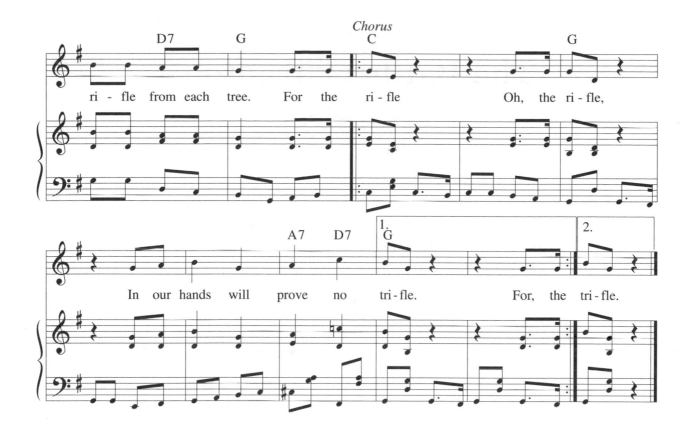

Ye ride a goodly steed,
Ye may know a goodly master,
Ye forward come with speed,
But you'll learn to back much faster
When you meet our mountain boys,
And their leader, Johnny Stark;
Lads who make but little noise,
Lads who always hit their mark. *Chorus*

Had ye no graves at home,
Across the briny water,
That hither ye must come,
Like bullocks to the slaughter?
Well, if we the work must do,
Then the sooner 'tis begun.
If flint and trigger hold but true,
The sooner 'twill be done. *Chorus*

The Riflemen of Bennington

The Battle of Trenton

Now to our station let us march and rendezvous with pleasure,
We have been like brave Minute Men to serve so great a treasure.
We let them see immediately that we are men of mettle,
We Jersey boys that fear no noise will never flinch from battle.
                                        — *"Song of the Minute Man"*

The British capture of Fort Washington on Manhattan Island on November 16, 1776, forced the American Army under General Washington to retreat through New Jersey and across the Delaware River into Pennsylvania. British General Sir William Howe posted the Hessian, Colonel Johannes Rall, and a contingent of about 1,200 mercenaries at Trenton, New Jersey. The main British force then went into winter quarters, leaving the Hessians unsupported. Washington, whose troops had been quietly reinforced, determined to take advantage of this lapse in British tactics. In an entry to his diary dated December 25, 1776, John Fitzgerald, an aide-de-camp to Washington, picks up the story:

> Christmas morning. They make a great deal of Christmas in Germany, and no doubt the Hessians will drink a great deal of beer and have a dance tonight. They will be sleepy tomorrow morning. Washington will set the tune for them about daybreak. The rations are cooked. New flints and ammunition have been distributed.

So it was that on the night of December 25, 1776, in the midst of a heavy snowstorm, Washington and his army rowed across the ice-choked Delaware River and, early the next morning, fell upon the Hessians, who were sleeping off their Christmas celebration. Taken completely by surprise, the enemy was overwhelmed and quickly surrendered. Coming after a long series of reverses, it was a much-needed victory for Washington and his men.

The Battle of Trenton

Our object was the Hessian band,
That dared invade fair freedom's land.
  And quarter in that place.
Great Washington he led us on,
Whose streaming flag in storm or sun,
  Had never known disgrace.

In silent march we passed the night,
Each soldier panting for the fight,
  Though quite benumbed with frost.
Greene, on the left, at six began,
The right was led by Sullivan,
  Who ne'er a moment lost.

Their pickets stormed, the alarm was spread,
The rebels risen from the dead
  Were marching in the town.
Some scampered here, some scampered there,
And some for action did prepare;
But soon their arms laid down.

Twelve hundred servile miscreants,
With all their colors, guns and tents,
  Were trophies of the day.
The frolic o'er, the bright canteen,
In center, front and rear was seen,
  Driving fatigue away.

Now, brothers of the patriot bands,
Let's sing deliverance from the hands
  Of arbitrary sway.
And as our life is but a span,
Let's touch the tankard while we can,
  In memory of that day.

The Liberty Song

I enclose you a song for American freedom. I have long since renounced poetry, but as indifferent songs are very powerful on certain occasions, I venture to invoke the deserted muses. I hope my good intentions will pardon, with those I please, for the boldness of my numbers . . .
—Excerpt from a 1768 letter from John Dickinson to Massachusetts anti-crown leader James Otis

John Adams attended a banquet on August 14, 1769, and wrote in his diary:

Dined with 350 Sons of Liberty in Robinson's Tavern in Dorchester. There was a large collection of good company. We had "The Liberty Song" (Dickinson's) and the whole company joined in the chorus.

Dickinson himself was somewhat ambivalent about American-British relations. His song calls upon Americans to give their money, not their lives, in the struggle for "liberty," not independence or separation. As a delegate to the Continental Congress in 1776, he actually voted against the Declaration of Independence, although when war broke out, he served in the Revolutionary Army.

The Liberty Song

Words by John Dickinson

Tune: "Hearts of Oak"

Come join hand in hand, brave A - mer - i - cans all, And
rouse your bold hearts at fair Lib - er - ty's call; No ty - ran - nous acts shall sup -

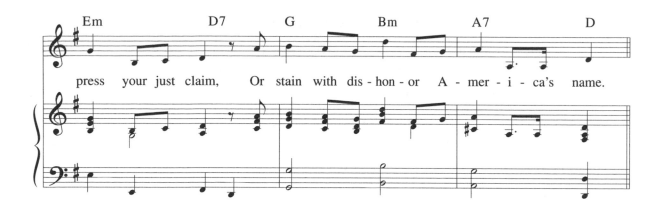

press your just claim, Or stain with dis-hon-or A-mer-i-ca's name.

Chorus

In free-dom we're born, and in free-dom we'll live. Our pur-ses are_ read-y.

Stead-y, friends, stead-y. Not as slaves,_ but as free-men, our mon-ey we'll give.

Our worthy forefathers - let's give them a cheer -
To climates unknown did courageously steer;
Through oceans to deserts, for freedom they came,
And dying, bequeathed us their freedom and fame.   *Chorus*

Their generous bosoms all dangers despised,
So highly, so wisely, their birthrights they prized;
We'll keep what they gave, we will piously keep,
Nor frustrate their toils on the land or the deep.   *Chorus*

The Tree their own hands had to Liberty reared.
They lived to behold growing strong and revered;
With transport they cried - "Now our wishes we gain,
For our children shall gather the fruits of our pains."   *Chorus*

How sweet are the labors that freemen endure,
That they shall enjoy all the profit, secure.
No more such sweet labors Americans know,
If Britons shall reap what Americans sow.   *Chorus*

Swarms of placemen and pensioners soon will appear,
Like locusts deforming the charms of the year.
Suns vainly will rise, showers vainly descend,
If we are to drudge for what others shall spend.   *Chorus*

The join hand in hard brave Americans all,
By uniting we stand, by dividing we fall.
In so righteous a cause let us hope to succeed,
For Heaven approves of each generous deed.   *Chorus*

All ages shall speak with amaze and applause
Of the courage we'll show in support of our laws.
To die we can bear - but to serve we disdain,
For shame is to freemen more dreadful than pain.   *Chorus*

This bumper I crown for our sovereign's health,
And this for Britannia's glory and wealth;
That wealth and that glory immortal may be,
If she is but just and we are but free.   *Chorus*

Yankee Doodle

The surest way to popularize an idea in song is to set new words to a familiar melody. As early as 1767, there was mention in Philadelphia of a comic song called "Yankee Doodle."

When the word "Yankee" first appeared in print, people were not quite sure just what it meant. To this day, there is some confusion about its origin. Some people believe it comes from an Indian word; others give it a French origin. The strongest possibility is that it comes from the Dutch name for the English colonists: *Jan Kaas* or *Jan Kees*. *Jan* is Dutch for "John"; *kees* means "cheese." "John Cheese" was not meant as a compliment. (The Dutch never quite got over their ouster from New Amsterdam by the English.) Neither was "Doodle," which refers to a fool.

"Yankee Doodle" first appeared in a London broadside in 1775. Its subtitle was "The Lexington March." The British band played it on its march to the Battle of Lexington, Massachusetts, on April 19 of that year. It was intended to cheer up the Redcoats and give them courage. But when the Minutemen heard the strains of the familiar tune, not only did it give away the British position, but it let them know that the British were mocking them by calling them "Yankee doodles."

In the true spirit of the times, the familiar melody was taken up by the Americans (with new words by a Harvard college student, Edward Bangs) and sung right back at them. It is this version of "Yankee Doodle" that has gone down in American history.

Bangs was a Minuteman who is said to have taken part in the actual fighting that day. We don't know exactly when he wrote the song, but at least one verse (verse seven) could not have been written before July 3, 1775. That was the day "Captain" George Washington took command of the American Army in Boston.

★ ★ ★ ★ ★ ★ ★ ★ ★ ★ ★ ★ ★ ★ ★ ★

A Saucy Verse

Yankee Doodle went to town,
Riding on a pony;
Stuck a feather in his cap
And called it macaroni.

This well-known verse doesn't seem to have anything to do with the rest of the song. Most people who sing it probably assume that it's just a bit of Revolutionary War nonsense. Not at all!

This verse was sung by the British to taunt the patriots. In eighteenth-century England, a "macaroni" was a gentleman who wore overly fancy clothes in what was perceived as the "Italian style," to try to make himself look more important than he really was. In other words, a macaroni was a dandy.

And just what was Yankee Doodle trying to do? He was, from the British point of view, getting "all dressed up" and "putting on airs." "Yankee Doodle" in this verse represents the Colonies and their foolish desire to be free of Great Britain.

★ ★ ★ ★ ★ ★ ★ ★ ★ ★ ★ ★ ★ ★ ★

Yankee Doodle

Words by Edward Bangs

Fath'r and I went down to camp, A - long with Cap - tain Good - ing, And there we saw a thou - sand men, As thick as hast - y pud - ding.

Chorus

Yan - kee Doo - dle keep it up, Yan - kee Doo - dle dan - dy.

Mind the mus - ic   and the step, And   with the girls be   hand - y.

And there we saw a thousand men
As rich as Squire David,
And what they wasted every day,
I wish it could be savéd. *Chorus*

And there we saw a swamping gun,
Large as a log of maple,
Upon a deucéd little cart,
A load for father's cattle. *Chorus*

And every time they shoot it off,
It takes a horn of powder.
It makes a noise like father's gun,
Only a nation louder. *Chorus*

Cousin Simon grew so bold,
I thought he would have cock'd it.
It scared me so, I shrieked it off,
And hung by father's pocket. *Chorus*

I saw a little barrel too,
The heads were made of leather.
They knocked on it with little clubs,
And called the folks together. *Chorus*

And there was Captain Washington,
And gentle folks about him.
They say he's grown so tarnal proud,
He will not ride without them. *Chorus*

He got himself in meeting-clothes,
Upon a slapping stallion.
He set the world along in rows,
In hundreds and in millions. *Chorus*

The flaming ribbons in his hat,
They looked so taring fine, ah,
I wanted pockily to get,
To give to my Jemimah. *Chorus*

The Revolutionary War

The War of 1812

The Star Spangled Banner

On the night of September 13–14, 1814, British naval forces undertook an intensive bombardment of Fort McHenry in Baltimore. Francis Scott Key (1779–1843) was a lawyer who was sent as an emissary to the British fleet in Chesapeake Bay just before the bombardment began to secure the release of a friend who had been captured by the British. The British commander, General Robert Ross, agreed to release the prisoner, but since the plans for the attack on Baltimore were well under way, he decided it would be prudent to keep both men on board. ("Loose lips can sink ships.") So it was that from the vantage point of the deck of a British man-o'-war, Key watched "the bombs bursting in air" over Fort McHenry. All through the night, the outcome of the bombardment was uncertain, but when the American flag could be seen still flying "by dawn's early light," it was apparent to Key, as well as to the British, that the attack had failed. While still on board, in a fever of inspiration, Key penned his immortal words. Released that day, he made a few revisions in a Baltimore hotel. The poem was published on September 20 in the *Baltimore Patriot* under the title "Defence of Fort M'Henry." Its setting to the familiar tune of "To Anacreon in Heaven" assured its widespread popularity—and even the ladies could sing it. (See the sidebar below.) It was subsequently adopted by the U.S. Army and Navy as "the national anthem," but when Congress officially proclaimed it the National Anthem on March 3, 1931, the quotation marks were removed for good.

What the Ladies Couldn't Sing

To Anacreon in heav'n, where he sat in full glee;
A few sons of harmony sent in a petition.
That he their inspirer and patron would be;

When this answer arrived from the jolly old Grecian:
  "Voice fiddle and flute,
  No longer be mute,
  I'll lend ye my name,
  And inspire ye, to boot.
And, besides, I'll instruct ye, like me, to entwine
The myrtle of Venus with Bacchus's vine."

Apollo rose up, and said: "Pr'y thee ne'er quarrel,
Good king of the gods, with my vot'ries below!
Your thunder is useless." Then shewing his laurel,
Cried, "Sic evitabile fulmen,* you know!
  Then over each head
  My laurels I'll spread.
  So my sons, from your crackers
  No mischief shall dread.
Whilst snug in their club-room, they jovially twine
The myrtle of Venus with Bacchus's vine."

* Thus you avoid lightning.

Unlikely as it may seem, Francis Scott Key's poem "The Star Spangled Banner" was adapted to the melody of this eighteenth-century ode to the Greek poet Anacreon (563–478 B.C.). The Anacreontic Society was an aristocratic drinking-and-singing club in London, and this was their "theme song." The song's popularity spread beyond the oak-paneled walls of the club's headquarters, and it was widely sung on both sides of the Atlantic. However, true gentlemen would never sing it in the presence of the ladies; its shocking references to Venus and Bacchus made it unsuitable for their delicate ears.

Anacreon's poetry was largely devoted to verses in praise

The War of 1812

of wine and love, or as the 1911 edition of *The Encyclopædia Britannica* so charmingly put it: "Anacreon has a reputation as a composer of . . . those bacchanalian and amatory lyrics which are commonly associated with his name." Small wonder, then, that this scandalous ode was deemed *hors de question* where the eighteenth-century ladies were concerned.

In the end, Anacreon was struck down by the *fulmen* (lightning) of his excesses. According to Pliny, at the age of eighty-five, he choked on a grape seed.

The Star Spangled Banner

Words by Francis Scott Key

Tune: "To Anacreon In Heaven"

The War of 1812

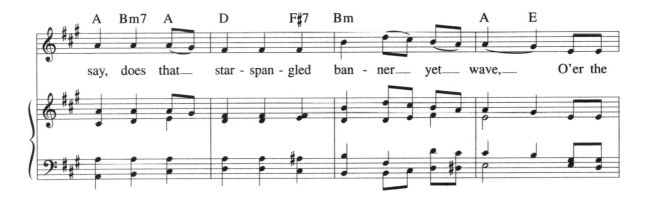

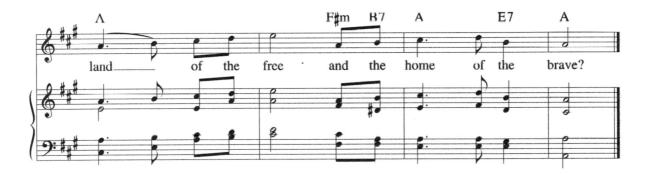

On the shore dimly seen through the mists of the deep,
Where the foe's haughty host in dread silence reposes,
What is that which the breeze, o'er the towering steep,
As it fitfully blows, half conceals, half discloses?
Now it catches the gleam of the morning's first beam,
In full glory reflected now shines on the stream.
'Tis the star-spangled banner, oh, long may it wave
O'er the land of the free and the home of the brave.

And where is the band that so vauntingly swore
That the havoc of war and the battle's confusion,
A home and a country shall leave us no more?
Their blood was washed out their foul footsteps's pollution.
No refuge could save the hireling and slave,
From the terror of death and the gloom of the grave.
And the star-spangled banner in triumph doth wave
O'er the land of the free and the home of the brave.

Oh, thus be it ever when freemen shall stand
Between their loved homes and the war's desolation;
Blessed with vic'try and peace, may the heaven-rescued land
Praise the power that hath made and preserved us a nation.
Then conquer we must, for our cause it is just,
And this be our motto: "In God do we trust."
And the star-spangled banner in triumph shall wave
O'er the land of the free and the home of the brave.

The War of 1812

Ye Parliament of England

In true traditional ballad style, this eleven-verse narrative recounts many of the principal naval engagements of the War of 1812, rattling off names of ships, battles, and heroes.

Commodore John Ro[d]gers was the commander of the frigate *President*. He served with distinction throughout the war.

Stephen Decatur was one of the outstanding U.S. naval commanders. He vanquished the H.M.S. *Macedonian* on October 25, 1812. He uttered the unforgettable toast: "Our country . . . may she always be right, but our country, right or wrong."

Verse five is a play on the name of the U.S.S. *Enterprise*, which beat the H.M.S. *Boxer* off Portland, Maine, on September 5, 1813. During this battle, both the American and British captains were killed.

Ye Parliament of England

The War of 1812

roused the sons of Lib - er - ty in North A - mer - i - cay.

You first confined our commerce and said our ships shan't trade,
You next impressed our seamen and used them as your slaves.
You then insulted Rogers while ploughing o'er the main,
And had we not declared war, you'd have done it o'er again.

You thought our frigates were but few, and Yankees could not fight,
Until bold Hull the *Guerrière* took, and banished her from sight.
The *Wasp* then took your *Frolic* - you nothing said to that.
The *Poictiers* being off the coast, of course you took her back.

Then next your *Macedonian*, no finer ship could swim,
Decatur took her gilt-work off, and then he took her in.
The *Java* by a Yankee ship was sunk, you all must know,
The *Peacock* fine, in all her prime, by Lawrence down did go.

Then next you sent your *Boxer* to box us all about,
But we had an "*Enterprising*" brig that beat your *Boxer* out;
We boxed her up to Portland and moored her off the town,
To show the sons of liberty this *Boxer* of renown.

Then next upon Lake Erie, brave Perry had some fun;
You own he beat your naval force and caused them for to run.
This was to you a sore defeat, the like ne'er known before.
Your British squadron beat complete, some took, some run ashore.

Then your brave Indian allies, you styled them by that name,
Until they turned their tomahawks, and by you, savages became.
Your mean insinuations they despised from from their souls,
And joined the sons of liberty that scorn to be controlled.

There's Rogers in the *President*, will burn, sink and destroy.
The *Congress*, on the Brazil, coast, your commerce will annoy.
The *Essex*, in the south seas, will put out all your lights;
The flag she waves at her mast-head: "Free Trade and Sailor's Rights."

Lament, ye sons of Britain, far distant is the day,
That e'er you'll gain what you have lost in North Americay.
Go tell your king and parliament, by all the world is known,
That British force, by sea and land's by Yankees overthrown.

Use every endeavor, and strive to make a peace,
For Yankee ships are building fast, their navy to increase.
They will enforce their commerce, the laws by heaven are made,
That Yankee ships, in time of peace, to any port may trade.

Grant us free trade and commerce and don't impress our men.
Give up all claims of Canada, then we'll be at peace again.
And then we will respect you and treat you as our friend;
Respect our flag and citizens, then all these wars will end.

Ye Parliament of England

Perry's Victory

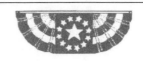

The most important battle of the War of 1812 was fought near Put-in-Bay in Lake Erie off the coast of Port Clinton, Ohio. There, on September 10, 1813, an American fleet commanded by Commodore Oliver Hazard Perry met and defeated a British squadron of six ships under the command of Captain Robert H. Barclay. As a result of Perry's triumph, the British were forced to evacuate Detroit, ultimately guaranteeing that the United States would not be compelled to cede any territory to Britain at the cessation of hostilities. Perry is remembered for this victory and for the famous message he sent to General William Henry Harrison ("Tippecanoe"): "We have met the enemy and they are ours; two ships, two brigs, one schooner and one sloop."

Perry's Victory

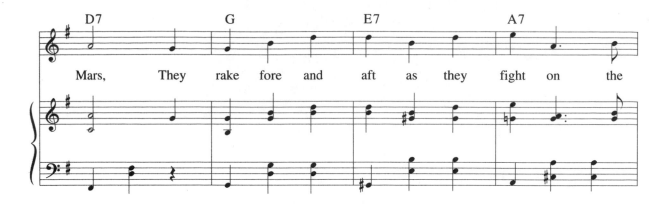

Mars, They rake fore and aft as they fight on the

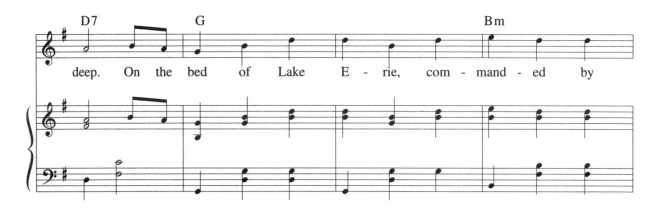

deep. On the bed of Lake E - rie, com - mand - ed by

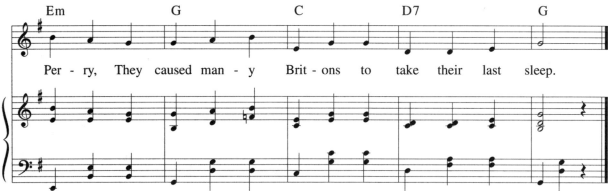

Per - ry, They caused man - y Brit - ons to take their last sleep.

The War of 1812

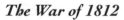

'Twas just at sunrise, and a glorious day,
Our squadron at anchor, snug in Put-in-Bay;
When we saw the bold Britons and cleared for a bout,
Instead of Put-in, by the Lord, we put out.
Up went the Union Jack, never up there before,
"Don't give up the ship," was the motto that it bore;
And as soon as that motto our gallant lads saw,
They thought of their *Lawrence** and shouted, "Huzza!"

O, then, 'twould have raised your hat three inches higher,
To see how we dashed in among them like fire;
The *Lawrence* went first, and the rest as they could,
And a long time the brunt of the battle she stood.
'Twas peppering work - fire, fury and smoke -
And groans, that from the wounded lads spite of them broke.
The water grew red round our ship as she lay,
Though 'twas never before so till that bloody day.

They fell around me, like spars in a gale,
The shot made a sieve of each rag of a sail;
And of our crew, scarce a dozen remained,
But these gallant tars still the battle maintained.
'Twas then our Commander - God bless his young heart! -
Thought it best from his well-peppered ship to depart,
And bring up the rest who were tugging behind
For why? They were sadly out of wind.

Then to Yarnall§ he gave the command of the ship,
And set out like a lark on his desperate trip
In a small open yawl, right through their whole fleet,
Who with many a broadside our cock-boat did greet.
I steered her and, damn me, if every inch
Of these timbers of mine at each crack didn't flinch.
But our tight little Commodore, cool and serene,
To move ne'er a muscle by any was seen.

Whole volleys of muskets were levelled at him,
But the devil a one ever grazed e'en a limb,
Though he stood up erect in the stern of the boat,
Till the crew pulled him down by the skirts of his coat.
At length, through Heaven's mercy, we reached the other ship,
And the wind springing up, we gave her the whip,
And ran down the line, boys, through thick and through thin,
And bothered their ears with a horrible din.

Then starboard and larboard, and this way and that,
We banged 'em and raked 'em and laid their masts flat;
Till one after t'other they hauled down their flag,
And an end put for that time to Johnny Bull's brag.
The *Detroit* and *Queen Charlotte* and *Lady Prevost*,
Not able to fight or to run, gave up the ghost;
And not one of them all from our grapplings got free,
Though we'd just fifty-four guns and they'd sixty-three.

Now give us bumper to Elliott‡ and those
Who came up in good time to belabor our foes;
To our fresh-water sailors we'll toss off one more,
And a dozen at least to our young Commodore.
And though Britons may talk of ruling the ocean,
And that sort of thing - by the Lord, I've a notion -
I'll bet all I'm worth - who takes it, who takes?
Though they're lords of the seas, we'll be lords of the Lakes.

*Perry's flagship.
§Lieutenant John J. Yarnell (his name is misspelled in the song), who was left in command of the Lawrence when Perry set out in a rowboat to take over command of the *Niagara* to continue the battle.
‡Lieutenant Jesse D. Elliott, commander of the *Niagara*.

Perry's Victory

The Hunters of Kentucky

Though Adams now misrules the land,
And strives t'oppress the free,
He soon must yield his high command
Unto "Old Hickory."

Then toast our Jackson, good and great,
The man whom we admire,
He soon will mount the chair of state,
Which patriots all desire.

Frontier "bragging" was very much an accepted form of expression in nineteenth-century America. Andrew Jackson's Kentucky riflemen liked to be thought of as "half horse—half alligator." This song details their exploits at the Battle of New Orleans (January 8, 1815) against British troops led by General Sir Edward Pakenham. It was used as a campaign song for Jackson in the three-way presidential election of 1824 between Jackson, Henry Clay, and John Quincy Adams. Although Jackson had a plurality in the popular vote, an electoral stalemate developed between the three candidates. Henry Clay, who felt that Jackson had usurped his claim to the "mantle of the West," finally cast his lot with Adams, making him the sixth president of the United States. Jackson's turn came four years later, when he defeated Adams in a bitterly fought contest.

Composer Samuel Woodworth's (1784–1842) best-known song is the sentimental "Old Oaken Bucket."

The Hunters of Kentucky

Words by Samuel Woodworth

Tune: "Unfortunate Miss Bailey"

Ye gen-tle men and la-dies fair who grace this fa-mous ci-ty, Just

lis-ten, if you've time to spare, while I re-hearse a dit-ty; And

The Hunters of Kentucky

49

for this op-por-tu-ni-ty con-ceive your-selves quite luck-y, For

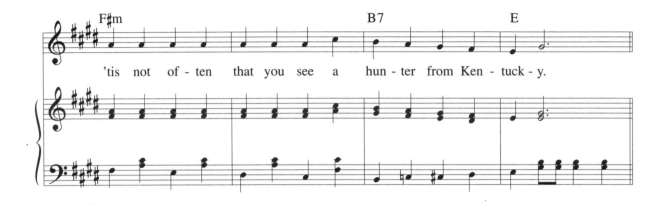

'tis not of-ten that you see a hun-ter from Ken-tuck-y.

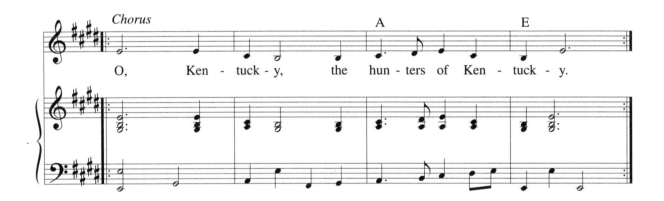

Chorus

O, Ken-tuck-y, the hun-ters of Ken-tuck-y.

The War of 1812

We are the hardy freeborn race,
Each man to fear a stranger;
Whate'er the game we join in chase,
Despoiling time and danger.
And if a daring foe annoys,
Whate'er his strength and forces,
We'll show him that Kentucky boys
Are alligator horses.   *Chorus*

I s'pose you read it in the prints,
How Pakenham attempted
To make Old Hickory Jackson wince,
But soon his scheme repented;
For we, with rifles ready cock'd,
Thought such occasion lucky,
And soon around the gen'ral flocked
The hunters of Kentucky.   *Chorus*

You've heard, I s'pose, how New Orleans
Is famed for wealth and beauty.
There's girls, it seems, of every hue,
From snowly white to sooty.
So Pakenham he made his brags,
If he in fight was lucky,
He'd have their girls and cotton bags,
In spite of Old Kentucky.   *Chorus*

But Jackson, he was wide awake,
And was not scared of trifles,
For well he knew what aim we take
With our Kentucky rifles.
He led us down to Cypress Swamp,
The ground was low and mucky.
There stood John Bull in all his pomp,
And here was old Kentucky.   *Chorus*

A bank was raised to hide our breasts,
Not that we thought of dying,
But that we always like to rest,
Unless the game is flying.
Behind it stood a little force,
None wished it to be greater,
For every man was half a horse
An half an alligator.   *Chorus*

They did not let our patience tire,
Before they showed their faces.
We did not choose to waste our fire,
So snugly kept our places.
But when so near we saw them wink,
We thought it time to stop 'em,
And 'twould have done you good, I think,
To see Kentuckians drop 'em.   *Chorus*

They found, at last, 'twas vain to fight,
Where lead was all the booty,
And so, they wisely took to flight,
And left us all our beauty.
And now, if danger e'er annoys,
Remember what our trade is;
Just send for us Kentucky boys,
And we'll protect ye, ladies.   *Chorus*

The Hunters of Kentucky

The *Constitution* and the *Guerrière*

The British Navy, beginning in 1799, found itself engaged in a life-and-death struggle for supremacy of the seas with Napoleon's fleet. Still smarting over the surrender of Cornwallis to Washington in 1783, and reacting to the Americans' sympathies with their former French allies, the Royal Navy began seizing American ships and impressing its seamen. By 1812, the situation had worsened enough so that on June 18, at the urging of President Madison, Congress declared war on Britain. Despite the firm conviction in the heart of every British tar that "Britannia rules the waves," the minuscule American Navy (sixteen ships versus hundreds flying the Union Jack) scored a series of startling victories, starting with the historic engagement between the U.S.S. *Constitution* and the British frigate *Guerrière* on August 19, 1812. Off the coast of Nova Scotia, the *Constitution,* commanded by Captain Isaac Hull, took just thirty minutes to completely vanquish the British ship, commanded by Captain James Dacres.

The *Constitution* and the *Guerrière*

It oft-times has been told, that Brit-ish sea-men bold, Could flog the tars of France so neat and han-dy - o! But they nev-er found their match, Till the Yan-kees them did catch. O, the

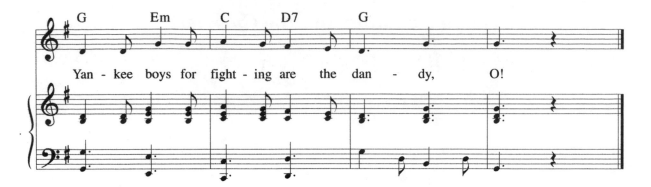

Yan-kee boys for fight-ing are the dan-dy, O!

The *Guerrière* a frigate bold,
On the foaming ocean rolled,
Commanded by proud Dacres, the grandee, O!
With as choice a British crew
As a rammer ever drew,
Could flog the Frenchman two to one so handy, O!

When this frigate hove in view,
Says proud Dacres to his crew,
"Come, clear ship for action, and be handy, O!
To the weather gage, boys, get her,"
And to make his men fight better,
Gave them to drink gunpowder mixed with brandy, O!

The Dacres loudly cries.
"Make this Yankee ship your prize.
You can in thirty minutes, neat and handy, O!
Twenty-five's enough, I'm sure,
And if you do it in a score,
I'll treat you to a double share of brandy, O!"

The British shot flew hot,
Which the Yankees answered not,
Till they got within distance they called handy, O!
"Now," says Hull unto his crew,
"Boys, let's see what you can do.
If we take this boasting Briton, we're the dandy, O!"

The first broadside we poured,
Carried her mainmast by the board,
Which made this lofty frigate look abandoned, O!
The Dacres shook his head,
And to his officers said,
"Lord! I didn't think the Yankees were so handy, O!"

Our second told so well,
That their fore and mizzen fell,
Which doused the royal enseign neat and handy, O!
"By George," says he, "we're done,"
And they fired a lee gun,
While the Yankees struck up "Yankee Doodle Dandy.

Then Dacres came on board
To deliver up his sword,
Though loath was he to lose it 'twas so handy, O!
"O! keep your sword." says Hull,
"For it only makes you dull.
Cheer up, and let us have a little brandy, O!"

Now fill your glasses full,
And we'll drink to Captain Hull,
And so merrily we'll push about the brandy, O!
John Bull may toast his fill,
But let the world say what they will,
The Yankee boys for fighting are the dandy, O!

The War of 1812

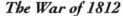

The Battle of New Orleans

The Battle of New Orleans was fought on January 8, 1812. It was the last major engagement of the War of 1812, but it need not have been fought at all. Unbeknownst to the combatants, the war had officially ended some two weeks earlier with the signing of the Treaty of Ghent between the Americans and the British. So British General Sir Edward Pakenham led his 5,300 troops against 4,500 firmly entrenched American sharpshooters under the command of Andrew Jackson in a doubly futile assault. In the half-hour battle, more than 2,000 British troops were killed or wounded, while the American casualties numbered 8 killed and 13 wounded. Pakenham himself died of his wounds. Jackson's fame as the "Hero of New Orleans" helped propel him into the White House in 1824.

The Battle of New Orleans

'Twas on the eighth of— Jan-u-a-ry, just at the dawn of day, We spied those Bri-tish— of-fi-cers all— dressed in battle a-ray. Old Jack-son then gave— or-ders: Each man to keep his

The War of 1812

post; And form a line from right to left, and let no time be lost.

With rockets and with bombshells, like comets we let fly;
Like lions they advanced us, the fate of war to try.
Large streams of fiery vengeance upon them we let pour,
While many a brave commander lay withering in his gore.

Thrice they marched up to the charge, and thrice they gave the ground.
We fought them full three hours, then bugle horns did sound.
Great heaps of human pyramids lay strewn before our eyes;
We blew the horns and rang the bells to drown their dying cries.

Come all you British noblemen and listen unto me -
Our frontiersman has proved to you America is free.
But tell your royal master when you return back home,
That out of thirty thousand men, but few of you returned.

Texas and Mexico, 1836–1848

Green Grow the Lilacs

This song highlights the mixed emotions of the soldier boy who feels patriotic in fighting his country's battles but longs for "the girl he left behind," who in this case seems to have found another "true love." So popular was the song with the troops from 1848 on that Mexicans began identifying Americans with its first two words, "green grow," which over time metamorphosed into "gringo," now a less-than-complimentary term for *norteamericano*.

Also known as "Green Grows the Laurel," this song dates back at least to the time of the wars of the Scottish Restoration in the late seventeenth century, when Scotsmen loyal to Bonnie Prince Charlie sang, "We'll change the green laurel to the bonnet so blue."

After the Mexican war, the song remained popular among cowboys, whose feelings about their own solitary lives were expressed in its lyrics. In 1931, Native American playwright Lynn Riggs wrote a play entitled *Green Grow the Lilacs*, which served as the inspiration for the musical *Oklahoma!*

Green Grow the Lilacs

Green grow the lilacs all spark-ling with dew, I'm lone-ly, my dar-ling, since part-ing with you. But by our next meet-ing, I hope to prove true, And change the green li-lacs to the red, white and blue.

Texas and Mexico, 1836–1848

I left my own true love to follow the flag,
For freedom for Texas - I don't like to brag.
To fight for my country, I'll have you to know,
To avenge our heroes in the Alamo.

I used to have a sweetheart, but now I have none,
Since she's gone and left me I care not for one.
Since she's gone and left me, contented I'll be,
For she loves another one better than me.

I passed my love's window both early and late,
The look that she gave me, it made my heart ache.
Oh, the look that she gave me was painful to see,
For she loves another one better than me.

I wrote my love letters in rosy red lines,
She sent me a letter all twisted in twines,
Saying, "Keep your love letters and don't waste your time,
Just you write to your love and I'll write to mine."

Green Grow the Lilacs

Remember the Alamo

Scots wha hae wi' Wallace bled,
Scots wham Bruce has often led,
Welcome to your gory bed,
Or to victory.
Now's the day and now's the hour,
See the front of battle lour,
See approach proud Edward's power,
Chains and slavery.

When the Alamo fell to Mexican General Santa Anna on March 13, 1836, the cry "Remember the Alamo" was taken up across our country. Its call to arms was memorably enshrined in this song, which borrows its melody from the song by Scottish poet Robert Burns, "Bruce's Address," also known as "Scots Wha Hae." For his poem, Burns drew inspiration from the Battle of Bannockburn, which took place on June 24, 1314. In that battle, Robert Bruce defeated the English under Edward II.

The Mexican Army had its own tune during its attack on the Alamo. Its band played *"Degüello"* ("Cut-Throat") as its troops stormed the Alamo and overwhelmed the fort's outnumbered defenders. Ten years later, when, after annexing Texas, General Zachary Taylor and his army defeated the Mexicans at the Battle of Monterrey on September 21–23, 1846, the song was sung with renewed fervor. Taylor culminated his exploits against Santa Anna (who by then was president of Mexico and commander-in-chief of its armed forces) the following year with a victory at Buena Vista. His troops called him "Rough and Ready," and that affectionate nickname served him in good stead in his successful run for the presidency in 1848.

Remember the Alamo

Words by T. A. Durriage

Tune: "Bruce's Address"

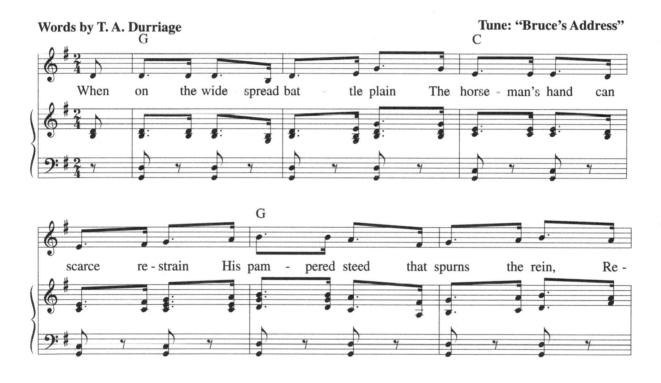

When on the wide spread bat - tle plain The horse - man's hand can scarce re - strain His pam - pered steed that spurns the rein, Re -

Heed not the Spanish battle yell,
Let every stroke we give them tell,
And let them fall as Crockett fell.
    Remember the Alamo!
For every wound and every thrust
On prisoners dealt by hands accursed
A Mexican shall bite the dust.
    Remember the Alamo!

The cannon's peal shall ring their knell,
Each volley sound a passing bell,
Each cheer Columbia's vengeance tell.
    Remember the Alamo!
For if, disdaining flight, they stand,
And try the issue hand to hand.
Woe to each Mexican brigand.
    Remember the Alamo!

Sung to last 8 measures

Then boot and saddle! Draw the sword!
Unfurl your banners bright and broad,
And as ye smite the murderous horde,
    Remember the Alamo!

Texas and Mexico, 1836–1848

Santy Anno

Antonio Lopez de Santa Anna (1795–1876) was, according to some accounts, "neither a general, nor a statesman, nor even an honest man, but he was the most conspicuous and continually active man of military adventures who filled Spanish America with violence during the first two decades of its independence." When the American settlers in Texas revolted and declared their independence from Mexico in 1836, Santa Anna led Mexican troops into battle against them, but was surprised and taken prisoner at San Jacinto on April 21, 1836. He might very well have been executed then and there for the vicious way in which he had conducted the war, but he was released on the condition that he order his troops to evacuate the country. Over the years, he was involved in numerous intrigues, both military and political. He became military dictator of Mexico in 1841, but was driven into exile in Cuba in 1845. By 1846, he was back in Mexico, having been recalled to command against the invading American Army. Defeated once more in 1848, he again went into exile, only to return in 1853 as president for life. In less than two years, however, he was overthrown and yet again had to flee the country. After that, he never regained his power or influence.

Santa Anna's quixotic misadventures made him the target of many a song and story north of the border. This sea shanty combines some of those stories with other bits of sailors' lore, particularly about sailing around Cape Horn to the gold fields of California.

Santy Anno

We're sail- ing down the riv - er from Liv - er - pool, Heave a -
way, San - ty An-no!_____ A - round Cape Horn to
Fris - co Bay, All___ on the plains of Mex - i - co.

Texas and Mexico, 1836–1848

So, heave her up and away we'll go,
Heave away, Santy Anno!
Heave her up and away we'll go,
All on the plains of Mexico.

General Scott and Taylor, too
Heave away, Santy Anno!
Made poor Santy meet his Waterloo,
All on the plains of Mexico.   *Chorus*

Santy Anno was a good old man,
Heave away, Santy Anno!
Till he got in a war with Uncle Sam,
All on the plains of Mexico.   *Chorus*

When Zachary Taylor gained the day,
Heave away, Santy Anno!
He made poor Santy run away,
All on the plains of Mexico.   *Chorus*

She's a fast clipper ship and a bully good crew,
Heave away, Santy Anno!
A down-east Yankee for her captain, too,
All on the plains of Mexico.   *Chorus*

Back in the days of 'forty-nine,
Heave away, Santy Anno!
Those were the days of the good old times,
All on the plains of Mexico.   *Chorus*

Santy Anno

The Song of Texas

By 1845, when this song first appeared, Americans were looking west to Oregon as well as south to Texas. Again, as in the settlement of Texas by Americans, the flow of American immigrants to that far northwestern corner caused no little agitation along a border. This time, America's "Manifest Destiny" bumped into Canada's view of its own sovereignty. The Democratic National Convention of 1844 declared that the title of the United States to "the whole territory of Oregon" was "clear and unquestionable." Leaving no latitude for compromise, the party made "Fifty-four forty or fight" a campaign slogan. However, once President Polk took office, a compromise over Oregon's northern border was struck. As a result of negotiations between American and Canadian envoys, the border was fixed somewhat farther south of the original demand, at the forty-ninth parallel.

In this rousing song, it is Texas itself that is singing in support of its future sister state of Oregon, which entered the Union in 1859.

The Song of Texas

free! And— when I shine a - mong the stars, How hap-py I will be!

Though Mexico in pride now,
Begins to threaten blows,
I'll grin at Sammy's side now,
With a thumb upon my nose. *Chorus*

In 'thirty-six I was of age,
Took Liberty's degrees,
And to unite I have a right,
With any state I please. *Chorus*

In Liberty's pure laws, now,
Uncle Sam and I are one,
And I will aid his cause now
For sister Oregon. *Chorus*

With Freedom's fire prolific,
We'll clear our rightful bound,
From Atlantic to Pacific
Is Uncle Sam's own ground. *Chorus*

    Last Chorus
The whole shall yet be free,
The whole shall yet be free.
And Uncle Sam shall have it all,
In peace and Liberty.

Texas and Mexico, 1836–1848

The Civil War

The Battle Cry of Freedom

"The Battle Cry of Freedom" was a hit song in every sense of the word, selling more than 350,000 copies of sheet music within two years of its introduction in a concert in Chicago on July 24, 1862. Its composer, George Frederick Root (1820–1895), was born in the small town of Sheffield, in the southwestern corner of Massachusetts, not far from the Connecticut state line. He showed an early interest in music and, after commencing his studies in Boston, went abroad to enrich his musical education in Paris. As a result of his classical European training, he wrote numerous cantatas and other "serious" works, none of which have survived the test of time. It was as a composer of popular songs that he really made his mark. And it was the outpouring of patriotic fervor during the Civil War that inspired him to create songs that have become enshrined in the history of that tragic conflict.

When at war's end the victorious Union flag was once again raised over Fort Sumter on April 14, 1865, it was hoisted to the strains of "The Battle Cry of Freedom." No composer could ever have wished for a greater honor.

A Union veteran recalled some years after the war the impression the song made on the troops stationed in Murfreesboro, Tennessee, after the nearby battle of Stones River, which began on December 31, 1862, and lasted until January 2, 1863. The night before the battle, the opposing armies encamped only a few hundred yards from each other. As a sort of overture to the killing that would begin the next day, the soldiers were treated to a "battle of the bands." The strains of "Yankee Doodle" and "Hail, Columbia" from the Union camp commingled with "Dixie" and "The Bonnie Blue Flag" from the Confederate side. Then an amazing thing happened: One of the bands struck up the universally popular, sentimental "Home, Sweet Home," which was immediately picked up (in the same key) by the musicians on the other side. Voices joined in, and soon thousands of mortal enemies were harmonizing on "Be it ever so humble, there's no place like home . . ." The war could have ended then and there, but unfortunately, it didn't.

The next morning, the battle was joined. Discord replaced harmony. After three days of bloody slaughter in which both sides suffered casualties of over 30 percent, the Confederate forces were compelled to withdraw in the face of increasing Union pressure. It was a "victory" for the North, but at a terrible price. Morale among the Union troops was low. One Union veteran remembered:

> By a happy accident, the glee club which came down from Chicago a few days afterward, brought with them the brand-new song, We'll Rally 'Round the Flag, Boys [sic] and it ran through the camp like wildfire. The effect was little short of miraculous. It put as much spirit and cheer into the camp as a splendid victory. Day and night you could hear it by every camp fire and in every tent. Never shall I forget how those men rolled out the line: "And although he may be poor, he shall never be a slave." I do not know whether Mr. Root ever knew what good work his song did for us there, but I hope so.

The Battle Cry of Freedom

Words and Music by George F. Root

Chorus

The Un-ion for - ev - er, Hur - rah, boys, hur-rah! Down with the trai - tor,

Up with the star; While we ral - ly 'round the flag, boys, ral - ly once a - gain,

Shout - ing the bat - tle cry of free - dom.

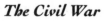

The Civil War

We are springing to the call of our brothers gone before,
　　Shouting the battle cry of freedom,
And we'll fill the vacant ranks with a million freemen more,
　　Shouting the battle cry of freedom.　*Chorus*

We will welcome to our numbers the loyal, true and brave,
　　Shouting the battle cry of freedom,
And although they may be poor not a man shall be a slave,
　　Shouting the battle cry of freedom.　*Chorus*

So, we're springing to the call form the East and from the West,
　　Shouting the battle cry of freedom,
And we'll hurl the Rebel crew from the land we love the best,
　　Shouting the battle cry of freedom.　*Chorus*

The Battle Hymn
of the Republic

John Brown's body lies a mouldering in the grave,
John Brown's body lies a mouldering in the grave,
John Brown's body lies a mouldering in the grave,
But his truth goes marching on.

Sergeant John Brown of Boston, a member of the Second Battalion, Boston Light Infantry, Massachusetts Volunteer Militia, was a member of his battalion's glee club. Upon his death, his singing comrades improvised verses about him to the tune of an old Methodist hymn.

Say, brothers, will you meet us,
Say, brothers, will you meet us,
Say, brothers, will you meet us,
On Canaan's happy shore?

When a certain other John Brown was hanged on December 2, 1859, for having led an unsuccessful raid on a government arsenal in Harper's Ferry, Virginia, the stage was set for a case of musical mistaken identity. This "mistake" produced not one but two of the most widely sung songs—not only of the Civil War, but in all of American history.

John Brown "number two" was a visionary abolitionist who had hoped to spark a slave insurrection by his band's attack on the arsenal. The failure of his foredoomed project and his subsequent execution captured the imagination of the entire nation. While the U.S. government regarded his deed as an act of insurrection, in the eyes of many he was a martyr who perished in a good cause. It was only natural, then, that people hearing the Massachusetts Militia glee club singing about "John Brown's body" would assume that the subject was the notorious abolitionist and not the unknown sergeant. The "folk process" took over, adding verses that glorified Brown number two and his courageous act.

> *He captured Harper's Ferry with his nineteen men so true,*
> *And he frightened "Old Virginny" till she trembled through and through.*
> *They hung him for a traitor, themselves a traitor crew,*
> > *His truth is marching on.*

> *John Brown died that the slaves might be free,*
> *John Brown died that the slaves might be free,*
> *John Brown died that the slaves might be free,*
> > *His truth is marching on.*

Enter Julia Ward Howe (1819–1910), a distinguished light of nineteenth-century literary society. Born in New York City, she began contributing poetry to New York periodicals at the age of sixteen. She wrote philosophical essays and, having moved to Boston after her marriage, delivered lectures on such weighty topics as "Doubt and Belief" and "The Duality of Character" before the Boston Radical Club and the Concord School of Philosophy. She advocated abolition and had met and admired John Brown some years before his name became a household word. Her progressive outlook on society led her to become one of the founders of the American Woman Suffrage Association and the Association for the Advancement of Women.

In the late autumn of 1861, Mrs. Howe accompanied her husband, Dr. Samuel Gridley Howe, a member of the Military Sanitary Commission appointed by President Lincoln, on an inspection tour of the Army camps around Washington. On one of the visits, Mrs. Howe and the others in her party began singing some of the popular war songs of the day along with the soldiers. Among the songs they sang was, of course, "John Brown's Body." It is safe to assume that nobody present had ever heard of the original John Brown. A member of the group, knowing of Mrs. Howe's poetical abilities, made the inspired suggestion that she write new words to the melody of "John Brown's Body." She thought it was a good idea.

> I replied that I had often wished to do so. In spite of the excitement of the day I went to bed and slept as usual, but awoke next morning in the gray of early dawn, and to my astonishment found that the wished-for lines were ar-

The Battle Hymn of the Republic

ranging themselves in my brain. I lay quite still until the last verse had completed itself in my thoughts, then hastily arose, saying to myself, "I shall lose this if I don't write it down immediately." I searched for an old sheet of paper and an old stump of a pen . . . and began to scrawl the lines almost without looking . . . Having completed this, I lay down again and fell asleep, but not without feeling that something important had happened to me.

Something important had happened—not only to her, but to the whole nation. What she had "scrawled without looking" that November in 1861 was published in February 1862 on the first page of the influential *Atlantic Monthly* magazine. (She was paid five dollars for her efforts.) The song was taken up and sung immediately. Its popularity spread like wildfire, in no small measure owing to the fact that its inspirational lyrics were set to the well-known, catchy tune. The song has endured in popularity over the 150 years since it was first composed.

The Battle Hymn of the Republic

Words by Julia Ward Howe

Music: "John Brown's Body"

I have seen Him in the watch fires of a hunderd circling camps;
They have builded Him an alter in the evening dews and damps;
I can read His righteous sentence by the dim and flaring lamps,
    His day is marching on.   *Chorus*

I have read a fiery gospel writ in burnished rows of steel;
"As ye deal with my contemners, so with you My Grace shall deal;
Let the hero, born of women, crush the serpent with his heel,"
    Since God is marching on.   *Chorus*

He has sounded forth the trumpet that shall never know retreat;
He is sifting out the hearts of men before His Judgement Seat;
Oh! be swift, my soul, to answer Him, be jubilant my feet!
    Our God is marching on!   *Chorus*

In the beauty of the lilies Christ was born across the sea,
With a glory in his bosom that transfigures you and me;
As he died to make men holy, let us die to make men free,
    While God is marching on.   *Chorus*

Lincoln and Liberty

I live for the good of my nation,
And my sons are all growing low;
But I hope the next generation
Will resemble old Rosin, the Beau.

The grand old Irish song "Old Rosin, the Beau" has had numerous American reincarnations. It surfaced as a campaign song for William Henry Harrison in the presidential election campaign of 1840 as "Old Tippecanoe." Harrison was called "Old Tippecanoe" by his supporters because he had commanded a detachment of American soldiers that defeated a band of Indians led by Tecumseh at the Battle of Tippecanoe Creek, Ohio, on November 7, 1811.

Harrison defeated the incumbent president, Martin Van Buren, in what was the first great "singing" presidential campaign. Not only did the Harrison camp create pro-Harrison songs, but they used the same tune to great effect with an anti–Van Buren song, "Little Vanny."

In 1844, as "Two Dollars a Day and Roast Beef," the song helped James K. Polk defeat Henry Clay.

In 1888, it worked for Benjamin Harrison against Grover Cleveland by evoking the memory of "Old Tippecanoe," Harrison's grandfather.

In 1892, in a rewrite called "Grandfather's Hat"—that again traded on Harrison's grandfather's name—it backfired. Cleveland won.

Turning back to the campaign of 1860 between Abraham Lincoln and Stephen Douglas, we find the nation on the brink of the Civil War. It had become apparent that a compromise between the North and the South could not be reached on the fundamental question of slavery and particularly on whether new states coming into the Union should be "free" or "slave." Passions had reached red-hot intensity when into the melee strode Jesse Hutchinson, patriarch of the famed Hutchinson Family Singers. For more than twenty years, the singing Hutchinsons had spread the message of Abolition and Temperance, first in their native New Hampshire and then, as their reputation grew, around the country. The Hutchinsons — Jesse, his wife, and children — wrote songs on an altogether different level from the typical mud-slinging ditties of the day.

It was only natural, therefore, that the Hutchinsons should ardently support the Lincoln campaign and presidency with their songs. Jesse drew upon the migrations of the Lincoln family in his lyrics to instill a sense of "native son" pride in the voters of three states: Lincoln was born in Kentucky, his family lived in Indiana, and his political career was based in Illinois. And what better melody to employ than the tried-and-true "Old Rosin, the Beau"?

Hutchinson refers to "Hoosierdom" and "Suckers" in the first verse of his song. "Hoosiers" are natives of Indiana; "Suckers" are natives of Illinois. Both terms supposedly arose from certain qualities or habits associated with these people. In the early Western settlements, men who prided themselves on their physical strength and ability to knock out their opponents were called "Hushers." On one occasion, a foreign-born riverboat man from Indiana apparently successfully dealt with several individuals at one time on the levee in New Orleans. After the fray, he loudly boasted in his accented English, "I'm a Hoosier!" The affair was reported in some New Orleans newspapers, and the term, originally applied only to boatmen from Indiana, came to be applied to all citizens of the state. As to "Suckers," the story goes that the Western prairies are full of little holes made by crayfish, which burrow down to reach the fresh water beneath. When the early settlers traversed the plains in what is now known as Illinois, they inserted long, hollow reeds into the holes and then sucked out the much-needed water.

Anyway, that's what they say.

Lincoln and Liberty

Words by Jesse Hutchinson

Music: "Old Rosin, the Beau"

son of Ken - tuck - y,_____ The he - ro of Hoo - sier - dom

through,_____ The pride of the "Suck - ers" so luck - y,

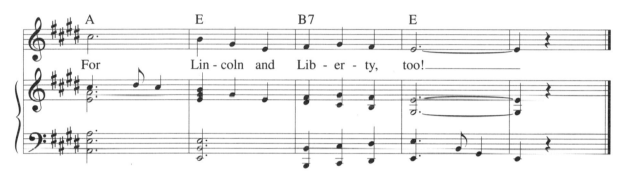

For Lin - coln and Lib - er - ty, too!_____

They'll find what by felling and mauling,
Our railmaker statesman can do;
For the people are everywhere calling
For Lincoln and Liberty, too.
    Then up with the banner so glorious,
    The star-spangled red, white and blue.
    We'll fight till our banner's victorious,
    For Lincoln and Liberty, too.

Our David's good sling is unerring,
The Slavocrat's giant he slew.
Then shout for the freedom preferring.
For Lincoln and Liberty, too.
    We'll go for the son of Kentucky,
    The hero of Hoosierdom through,
    The pride of the "Suckers" so lucky -
    For Lincoln and Liberty, too.

Lincoln and Liberty

Roll, *Alabama*, Roll

Fare you well, the Prince's landing stage,
River Mersey, fare you well.
I'm off to Califor-ni-a,
A place I know right well.

So, fare you well, my own true love,
When I return, united we will be.
It's not the leaving of Liverpool that grieves my mind,
But, my darling, when I think of thee.

Birkenhead, a hamlet whose population was 50 in 1818, lies on the banks of the Mersey River opposite the city of Liverpool, England. It was there that in 1824, William Laird purchased a few acres of land on the banks of a marshy stream known as Wallasey Pool that flowed into the Mersey River about two miles west of the village. Laird wanted to convert Wallasey Pool into a great shipbuilding basin, but his project was fiercely opposed by shipping interests in Liverpool, who feared the potential competition of this newcomer to their domain. It was not until 1847, four years after Liverpool's objections had been overcome by an act of Parliament, that the Birkenhead docks were finally completed. In 1861, Prince Albert, husband of Queen Victoria, died and the docks were renamed in his memory.

When the Civil War broke out in the United States, the Confederacy had some experienced naval officers who had seen service in the U.S. Navy, but it had no navy of its own. In preparation for an attempt to break the Union blockade that would surely strangle the South, Confederacy officials sent agents to England and France to try to purchase ships.

British textile mills had relied heavily on Southern cotton. The Union strategy was obvious: prevent the shipment of Southern cotton to England and thereby impose severe economic hardship upon the Confederacy. Liverpool (and Birkenhead) strongly supported the Southern cause, for sentimental as well as economic reasons. As a contemporary American observer remarked: "Liverpool was made by the slave trade, and the sons of those who acquired fortunes in the traffic now instinctively side with the rebelling slave-drivers."

So it was that when Southern agent James D. Bulloch was dispatched to the Liverpool shipyards to order the construction of blockade-running ships, he was warmly welcomed by local shipbuilders, despite Britain's Foreign Enlistment Act, which forbade the construction and arming of warships in British territory for a belligerent power. The *Alabama* was constructed in the Laird shipyard in 1862 and during the next two years, it created havoc for Union shipping, sinking over sixty-four merchant vessels. Recounting an engagement that took place on January 11, 1863, between the Union gunboat *Hatteras* and the *Alabama*, a Southern balladeer sang:

> *Off Galveston, the Yankee fleet, secure at anchor lay,*
> *Preparing for a heavy fight they were to have next day*
> *Down came the* Alabama, *like an eagle o'er the wave,*
> *And soon the gunboat* Hatteras *had found a watery grave.*

But a watery grave lay in store for the *Alabama* as well. On June 19, 1864, the Union man-of-war U.S.S. *Kearsarge* finally trapped the *Alabama* in the harbor of Cherbourg, France, where it had sought refuge. Word of the impending battle reached England and spread across France. Parisians flocked to the coast and British yachtsmen sailed across the English Channel to witness the exciting spectacle. Finally, with his "honor" at stake, Captain Raphael Semmes sailed the *Alabama* out of the harbor to do battle with the waiting *Kearsarge,* commanded by his former cabin mate Captain John Winslow.

> *The* Alabama *she is gone,*
> *She'll cruise the seas no more.*
> *She met the fate that she deserved*
> *Along the Frenchman's shore.*
> *Then here is luck to the* Kearsarge,
> *We know what she can do,*
> *Likewise to Captain Winslow*
> *And to his gallant crew.*

> ### Roll, Alabama, Roll

Roll, *Alabama*, Roll

When the Al - a - ba - ma's keel was laid,—— Roll, Al - a - ba - ma, roll, 'Twas——

laid in the yard of Jon - a-than Laird, Oh, roll, *Al - a - ba - ma,* roll.

'Twas laid in the yard of Jonathan Laird,
  Roll, *Alabama,* roll
'Twas laid in the town of Brikenhead,
  Oh, roll, *Alabama,* roll

Down the Mersey ways she rolled then,
  Roll, *Alabama,* roll.
Liverpool fitted her with guns and men,
  Oh, roll, *Alabama,* roll.

From the Western Isles she sailed forth,
  Roll, *Alabama,* roll.
To destroy the commerce of the North,
  Oh, roll, *Alabama,* roll.

To Cherbourg port she sailed one day,
  Roll, *Alabama,* roll.
To take her count of prize money,
  Oh, roll, *Alabama,* roll.

Many a sailor lad he saw his doom,
  Roll, *Alabama,* roll.
When the *Ke-arsage* it hove in view.
  Oh, roll, *Alabama,* roll.

'Til a ball from the forward pivot that day.
  Roll, *Alabama,* roll.
Shot the *Alabama*'s stern away.
  Oh, roll, *Alabama,* roll.

Off the three-mile limit in sixty-five,
  Roll, *Alabama,* roll.
The *Alabama* went to her grave.
  Oh, roll, *Alabama,* roll.

Roll, Alabama, *Roll*

Tenting on the Old Camp Ground

There are bonds of all sorts in this world of ours;
Fetters of friendship and ties of flowers,
And true lovers' knots, I ween.
The boy and the girl are bound by a kiss,
But there's never a bond, old friend, like this:
We have drunk from the same canteen.

When Walter Kittredge received his draft notice from the Union Army in 1863, his immediate response was to write "Tenting on the Old Camp Ground." Perhaps he imagined himself far from home on some lonely and devastated battlefield. However, when he reported for his preinduction physical, he was rejected as unfit for military service because of a childhood bout with rheumatic fever. He then did the next best thing: he had his song published.

At first, Kittredge had difficulty finding a publisher in his native Boston. The publishers there felt that the song was too depressing; the spirit of the times, they said, called for something more rousing and uplifting. Songs that called for an end to the war "wouldn't sell," they believed. But Kittredge had another, natural outlet for his song. He had been a member of one of the Hutchinson Family singing groups. The Hutchinsons were so successful and popular that they actually had a number of ensembles touring and performing their repertoire under their name. Asa Hutchinson, son of the group's founder, Jesse, had his singers introduce Kittredge's song in a series of concerts they presented near Lynn, Massachusetts. The audience reaction was enthusiastically positive. Apparently, Kittredge was not the only person "wishing for the war to cease."

Buoyed by the popular acclaim of the song, Asa had no difficulty convincing Boston publisher Oliver Ditson Company to issue it. The song was as popular among the

Southern soldiers as it was with the Union troops. The general population on both sides of the Mason-Dixon Line also instantly related to it. A tribute to the song is that it was never turned into a "Southern" song. Although it eventually was published in the South with a different set of verses (for no apparent reason—the replacement verses expressed essentially the same sentiments), its chorus remained unchanged; all the soldiers felt the same way about "dying on the old camp ground."

Kittredge was never able to match the success of this song with any of the many other songs he wrote after the war.

Tenting on the Old Camp Ground

Words and music by Walter Kittredge

We're tent - ting to - night on the old camp ground, Give us a song to

cheer Our wear - y hearts, a song of home, And friends we love so dear.

Chorus

Man - y are the hearts that are wear - y to-night, Wish - ing for the war to

The Civil War

96

We've been tenting tonight on the old camp ground,
Thinking of days gone by,
Of the loved ones at home that gave us a hand,
And the tear that said, "Goodbye." *Chorus*

We are tired of war on the old camp ground,
Many are dead and gone,
Of the brave and true who've been their homes,
Others been wounded long. *Chorus*

We've been fighting today on the old camp ground,
Many are lying near;
Some are dead and some are dying,
Many are in tears. *Chorus*

Tenting on the Old Camp Ground

When Johnny Comes Marching Home

With your guns and drums and drums and guns, huroo, huroo,
With your guns and drums and drums and guns, huroo, huroo,
With your guns and drums and drums and guns, the enemy nearly slew ye.
Oh, my darling dear, ye look so queer, och, Johnny, I hardly knew ye.

The Irish song "Johnny, I Hardly Knew Ye" bears a strong resemblance to "When Johnny Comes Marching Home" in both form and tune. The song is a tragic ballad about a young Irishman who was conscripted into the British Army and shipped off to fight for the Crown in far-off Ceylon, then returned home to his wife a blinded cripple.

I'm happy for to see ye home, huroo, huroo,
I'm happy for to see ye home, huroo, huroo,
I'm happy for to see ye home, all from the island of Ceylon,
So low in flesh, so high in bone, och, Johnny, I hardly knew ye.

In attempting to ascertain which song came first, we noted that British troops were first sent to fight the Dutch occupiers of Ceylon in 1795. Three years later, a popular rebellion again necessitated British military intervention, and Irish regiments were extensively recruited for the East India service. There were other outbreaks of fighting in 1817, 1843, and 1848, but since then, according to official documents, "the political atmosphere of Ceylon has remained undisturbed."

We can infer from this that the Irish song predates the American one. What else can we say about the origins of the "Civil-War Johnny"?

The first printed version of "When Johnny Comes Marching Home" was inscribed: "Music introduced in the Soldier's Return March By Gilmore's Band—Words & Music by Louis Lambert." "Louis Lambert" was the *nom de plume* of Patrick S. Gilmore, band-master of the Union Army attached to General Butler's command in New Orleans. He was born in Ireland on December 25, 1829, and could very well have found himself on a British troop ship bound for Ceylon in 1848 if it were not for the fact that he had emi-grated to America sometime earlier to escape the potato famine and conscription.

Developing his musical gifts, which had already manifested in Ireland, Gilmore em-barked on a musical/military career, the culmination of which, as just mentioned, was his appointment as bandmaster for the U.S. Army. In the postwar years, he organized so-called Monster Peace Jubilees, which featured orchestras of 1,000 musicians and cho-ruses of 10,000 voices.

As to the origins of Gilmore's song, which he claimed to have composed (not that any doubts were ever expressed in his lifetime), it is certainly reasonable to suppose that he may have heard the Irish version, or something akin to it, in his native land. Composers have always reached into the folk expression of their people for inspiration, sometimes without being consciously aware of it. The common name "Johnny" often symbolized the young soldier boy (such as in the "Yan" of "Yankee Doodle"; "Johnny Reb," the nick-name for Confederate soldiers; and "Johnny, Get Your Gun," a World War One song), until the emergence of GI Joe in World War Two.

"When Johnny Comes Marching Home" was an immediate success during the Civil War and its aftermath, but its popularity reached its height during the Spanish-American War in 1898. Since then, the song has continually figured in memorial and celebratory concerts around the country.

When Johnny Comes Marching Home

Words and Music by Patrick S. Gilmore

The Civil War

☆ ☆

100

men will cheer,— the boys will shout, The la - dies, they— will all turn out, And we'll all feel gay When John - ny comes march - ing home.—

The old church bell will peal with joy,
   Hurrah, hurrah!
To welcome home our darling boy,
   Hurrah, hurrah!
The village lads and lasses say
With roses they will strew they way,
And we'll all feel gay,
When Johnny comes marching home.

Get ready for the jubilee,
   Hurrah, hurrah!
We'll give the hero three times three,
   Hurrah, hurrah!
The laurel wreath is ready now
To place upon his loyal brow,
And we'll all feel gay,
When Johnny comes marching home.

Let love and friendship on that day,
   Hurrah, hurrah!
Their choices treasures then display,
   Hurrah, hurrah!
And let each one perform some part,
To fill with joy the warrior's heart,
And we'll all feel gay,
When Johnny comes marching home.

When Johnny Comes Marching Home

World War One

Over There

By the time America entered World War One in 1917, Tin Pan Alley songwriters had already composed a great number of patriotic, sentimental, humorous, pro- and anti-war songs, with titles such as "The War in Snider's Grocery Store," "I Didn't Raise My Boy to Be a Soldier," "When the *Lusitania* Went Down," "Shrapnel Bag," and "Somewhere in France." With few exceptions, most of these songs have faded from memory, but one—"Over There"—has withstood the test of time and is as pertinent and recognizable today as it was when George M. Cohan first penned it in 1917.

Cohan (1878–1942) was the great all-around song-and-dance man of his time. In his more than fifty years in show business, beginning as a child performer with his actor parents, he wrote 40 plays, collaborated with others on another 40 plays, and shared the production of still another 150 plays. He made over 1,000 appearances as an actor. Some of the more than 500 songs that he wrote were major national hits. Among these songs were "Give My Regards to Broadway," "Mary's a Grand Old Name," "Forty-Five Minutes From Broadway," "You're a Grand Old Flag," and "The Yankee Doodle Boy." Of all of Cohan's musical successes, however, nothing approached the popularity of "Over There," which ranked alongside the British "It's a Long Way to Tipperary" (which had actually been composed in 1912) as the outstanding "hit" of World War One.

Cohan composed "Over There" during the course of a forty-five-minute commuter-train ride from his home in suburban New Rochelle to New York City. Incidentally, that commute also served as the inspiration for one of Cohan's musicals, aptly titled "Forty-Five Minutes From Broadway."

Twenty-five years later, during World War Two, Congress authorized President Franklin Delano Roosevelt to present Cohan with the Congressional Medal of Honor for this inspiring song. The song had as much significance the second time around as it had had the first.

Over There

Words and Music by George M. Cohan

John - nie get your gun, get your gun, get your gun, Take it on the run, on the
John - nie get your gun, get your gun, get your gun, John - nie show the Hun, you're a

run, on the run; Hear them call - ing you and me;
son - of - a - gun. Hoist the flag and let her fly,

Ev - 'ry son of lib - er - ty. Hur - ry right a - way, no de-
Like true he - roes, do or die. Pack your lit - tle kit, show your

coming, the Yanks are coming, The drums rum - tum-ming ev - 'ry-where. _

So pre - pare, _ say a pray'r, _ Send the word, send the

word to be - ware. _ We'll be o - ver, we're com - ing o -

ver, And we won't come back till it's o - ver o - ver there. there.

The Fighting Sixty-Ninth

On the twenty-first of July,
Beneath the burning sun,
McDowell met the Southern troops
In battle at Bull Run;
Above the Union vanguard
Was proudly dancing seen,
Beside the starry banner,
Old Erin's flag of green.
Colonel Corcoran led the Sixty-Ninth
On that eventful day,
I wish the Prince of Wales were there
To see him in the fray.

New York's "Irish Brigade," the "Fighting 69th" ("Gentle when stroked. Fierce when provoked."), was organized in 1851 as a militia whose primary task was to protect their new homes and families against the anti-Irish violence that threatened their daily lives. When the Civil War broke out ten years later, they answered Lincoln's call for volunteers and served heroically in the Army of the Potomac. In fighting for the Northern cause against the South, which was supported by England, they felt they were doing double duty: fighting for their new homeland and fighting against their traditional oppressors. This is the reason for the oblique reference to the Prince of Wales in the above verse and for the even more pointed reference in the verse below:

When the Prince of Wales came over here and made a hubbaboo,
Oh, everybody turned out, you know, in gold and tinsel too;
But then the good old Sixty-Ninth didn't like these lords or peers —

They wouldn't give a damn for kings, the Irish volunteers!
We love the land of Liberty, its laws we will revere,
"But the divil take nobility!" say the Irish volunteers.

When the United States entered World War One on April 6, 1917, the 69th's record of service had been further embellished by action in the Spanish-American War in 1898 and in the Texas border campaign against Pancho Villa in 1916. The regiment was still predominantly Irish Catholic, but not exclusively so. Reflecting the changing times, such non-Irish names as Beliveau, Rodriguez, Guida, Ivanowski, Jaeger, and Kirk answered "present" to the roll call. The 69th, now renamed the 165th Infantry, became part of the 42nd "Rainbow Division," which consisted of National Guard units from twenty-six states and the District of Columbia. Surveying his men, its chief of staff, Major (later General) Douglas MacArthur, remarked that the division stretched like a rainbow, covering the country from one end of the sky to the other. MacArthur's poetic image of a rainbow was adopted as the name of the division, and MacArthur eventually rose to command the division.

By December 1917, the regiment found itself stationed in France, in the old Roman town of Grand. Christmas mass was celebrated by the regimental chaplain, Father Duffy (whose memorial statue was subsequently erected in New York City's Times Square). The next morning (December 26), the men marched off down a road built by Caesar's legions, on their way to their assigned area, Longeau. Underfed, underclothed, and poorly shod, they hiked through a blizzard over passes in the Vosges Mountains for four days and four freezing nights. According to one medical officer, the march "made Napoleon's retreat from Moscow look like a Fifth Avenue parade." No one fell out of line voluntarily despite the extreme conditions. Only those who fell unconscious from exhaustion were picked up by ambulances following the march.

The 165th Infantry took part in some of the bloodiest fighting of the war, suffering 3,501 casualties: 644 killed in action and 2,857 wounded. It participated in campaigns in Lorraine, Champagne, Champagne-Marne, Aisne-Marne, St. Mihiel, and Meuse-Argonne.

After the armistice, the regiment participated in the occupation of Germany. The men ended their duty on the Rhine River, remembered by some as the "Ryan."

On April 28, 1919, the Fighting 69th proudly marched up Fifth Avenue in the victory parade on "the sidewalks of New York." Colonel Donovan ordered his men to wear their helmets, leggings, and fixed bayonets as they would if they were marching off to combat. He said to them: "They won't see your faces, but they will remember what you look like."

World War One

The Fighting Sixty-Ninth

Words and Music by Anna L. Hamilton

We're not a war-ring na-tion, but we had to take a stand, To
ma-ny of the Six-ty-Ninth have nev-er been to war, But

help the oth-er na-tions and to save our na-tive land. Now Un-cle Sam is
nev-er on a bat-tle-field were brav-er troops be-fore. A-mid the shot and

rcad-y, read-y for the fray; So he sends the fight-ing Six-ty-Ninth to
shell, they will fight like hell. So give three cheers for the gal-lant boys of the

France to win the day.
fight-ing Six - ty Ninth.

Chorus They'll fight, fight, fight, be-cause they know that they are

right. They'll fight, fight, fight, Yes, they'll fight with all their might. They'll

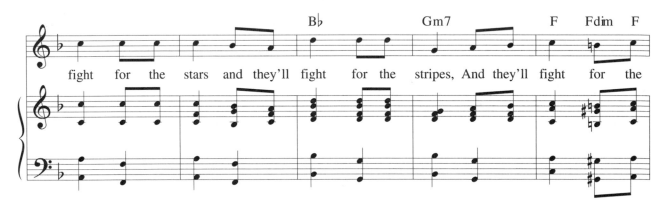

fight for the stars and they'll fight for the stripes, And they'll fight for the

o - pen seas. Three cheers for the Red, White and

Blue. _____ Three _____ cheers for the Tri - co - lor too. _____

_____ Yes, they'll fight, they will fight for France with all _____ of their might, And they'll

die for the Red, White and Blue. _____ Now

Coast Artillery Song

The "Coast Artillery Song" was published in *The Army Song Book*, which was supplied by the Commission on Training Camp Activities. The tune is taken from the traditional Irish song "Rambling Wreck of Poverty," which has served as an inspiration over and over on both sides of the Atlantic for songs such as the Georgia Tech school song, "I'm a Rambling Wreck From Georgia Tech," and Woody Guthrie's "Biggest Thing That Man Has Ever Done."

Marshall French (mentioned in verse three) is John Denton Pinkstone French (1852–1925), First Earl of Ypres. He earned that illustrious title in recognition of his service as commander of the British Army from the outbreak of the war until the end of 1915 and in particular for his involvement in the Battle of Ypres in May 1915. In reality, the coast artillery had nothing to do with Battle of Ypres, as it occurred some two years before America entered the war. So, what we have here is an Anglo-American pastiche involving the "President," the "king," and the "kaiser."

Coast Artillery Song

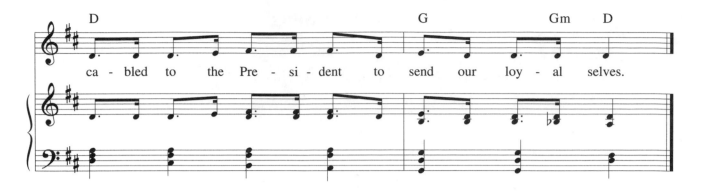

ca - bled to the Pre - si - dent to send our loy - al selves.

Chorus
Then, it's home, boys, home, it's home that we should be.
It's home, boys, home, when the nation shall be free.
We're in this war until it ends, and Germany will see
That the end of all the kaisers is the Coast Artillery.

When British Tommies took the field to stop the barb'rous Hun,
They found their light artillery was beaten gun for gun.
So Marshall French got on the wire and quickly told the king
That the garrison artillery would be the only thing. *Chorus*

So, limber up the sixes and tens and other guns,
And bracket on the O. T. line until you get the Huns.
There may be many plans and schemes to set this old world free,
But you'll find in every one a part for coast artillery. *Chorus*

Goodbye Broadway,
Hello France

Composed when America entered World War One in 1917, this song is a typical example of the rousing, toe-tapping tunes that sent the doughboys off to the trenches in France. It served to raise the spirits of the young men who were soon to experience the horrors "over there," while at the same time cheering the folks on the home front.

Goodbye Broadway, Hello France

Words by C. Francis Riesner & Benny Davis

Music by Billy Baskette

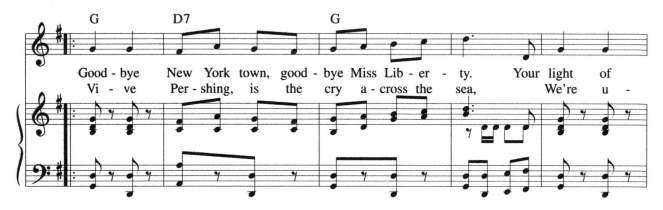

Good - bye New York town, good - bye Miss Lib - er - ty. Your light of

Vi - ve Per - shing, is the cry a - cross the sea, We're u -

Goodbye Broadway, Hello France

119

Chorus

Good-bye Broad-way, Hel-lo France,_____ We're ten mil-lion

strong._____ Good-bye sweet-hearts, wives and moth-ers,

It won't take us long._____ Don't you wor-ry

while we're there,— It's for you we're fight-ing too._____ So,

World War One

Keep Your Head Down, "Fritzie Boy"

Inspired by a Brave Tommy and Written at the Battle of Ypres, 1915

Gitz Rice was a member of the Canadian Army who fought alongside the American and British troops in France. His wartime compositions were as popular with the doughboys as with the Tommies. They include such numbers as "We Stopped Them at the Marne," "I Want to Go Home," and the familiar "Mademoiselle From Armentières (Parlez-vous)."

Keep Your Head Down, "Fritzie Boy"

Words and Music by Lieut. Graham "Gitz" Rice

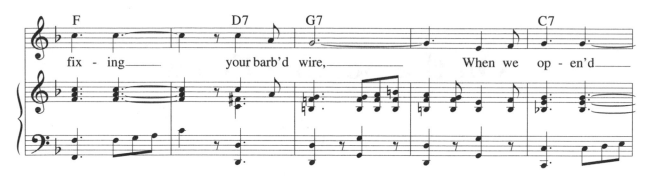

fix - ing_____ your barb'd wire,_____ When we op-en'd_____

_ 'rap - id fire!'_____ If you want to see your 'Vat - er' in the

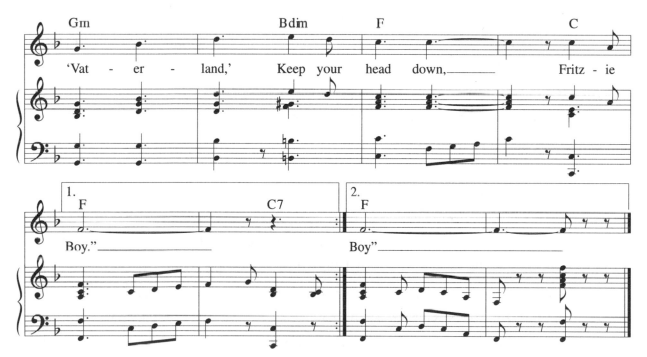

'Vat - er - land,' Keep your head down,_____ Fritz - ie

1.
Boy."_____

2.
Boy"_____

On the Somme Front

The first battle along the Somme River in northern France was a protracted series of Franco-British offensives during the latter half of 1916. On the morning of July 1, after an intense artillery bombardment of the German defenses, the British infantry went over the top in close-packed waves at a slow walk in strict alignment. They had not learned their lessons during the French and Indian War and at Lexington and Concord. They were mowed down by German machine guns. By July 15, the campaign had degenerated into a campaign of attrition. On September 15, the French launched an attack designed to take the pressure off the British. Then the weather turned rainy and "General Mud" stalled the advance. When the weather cleared up, the last assault was undertaken on November 13. The gains were measured in yards, while the casualties were counted in thousands.

The second battle was launched by the Germans on March 21, 1918. It marked the last great series of German offensives of the war. American reserves joined the British and French under the supreme command of French General Ferdinand Foch. By March 30, the German attack had been stalled in especially bloody fighting. The British suffered grievously: about 200,000 casualties and 190,000 prisoners taken by the Germans. The German casualties were about 180,000. Despite these terrible losses, a major Allied counteroffensive from July to November 1918 drove the German forces back to the Hindenburg line, which was broken through in September, leading to a final victory for the Allies.

On the Somme Front

Words by Joseph O'Connor

Music by Private J. Tavender

The U. S. A. gave up her ver-y best sons, To take those Ger-mans'
Can-a-da gave up their fin-est men to fight, To teach those Prus-sians that

trench-es and guns; While sis-ters and broth-ers so fond and true,
Right is Might; While mo-thers and wives dear, so fond and true,

We're Going to Celebrate the End of the War in Ragtime

It was 1915 and America was two years away from entering World War One. Still, that didn't stop songwriters from expressing their sentiments about the titanic struggle going on "over there." The strains of "It's a Long, Long Way to Tipperary," which had originally been written in 1912 as a British music-hall number about a young, homesick Irishman in London writing a letter to his "Irish Molly" back home, had taken on new meaning. An American "sequel" was entitled "It May Be Far to Tipperary (It's a Longer Way to Tennessee)." Other musical evidence of our growing emotional involvement was echoed in songs such as "When the *Lusitania* Went Down" and "Joan of Arc, They're Calling You."

Meanwhile, Tin Pan Alley was caught up in the ragtime craze. Syncopation was sweeping the nation. Many songs tried to come to grips with the reality of the situation, only to treat the matter in a lighthearted vein, as evidenced by "Shrapnel Rag":

> *Hear that shell, ain't it hell,*
> *When they start to shooting with shrapnel!*
> *Day and night, in the fight,*
> *The boys must keep a-ducking to the left and right.*
> *Dukes and Czars in armored cars,*
> *Going to the front a-puffing big cigars.*
> *Oh! you kid, they surely skip and skid,*
> *A-dodging the shooting stars.*
>
> *Oh, it's the "shrapnel rag,"*
> *An international snag.*
> *All those nutty nations now are doing it.*

Every ruined nation now is ruing it.

And the neutral nations are eschewing it.

Oh, it's the shrapnel rag,

And not their countries' flag,

So the wounded devils now are viewing it.

Diplomats and Democrats discussing it.

Emp'rors, Kings and Presidents are cussing it.

It's all the same,

No matter who is to blame,

Scrapping 'neath the shrapnel rag.

The second verse heightens the sense of unreality:

Holy gee! Look and see

What a forty centimeter did to me.

It's all the same who took aim,

I fear for sev'ral days I'll be a little lame.

Aeroplanes and armored trains

Cannot stand the traffic when the shrapnel rains.

Then lift your lids to the cannon, kids,

They have to stand the shooting pains.

Oh, it's the shrapnel rag . . .

We're Going to Celebrate the End of the War in Ragtime

Words and Music by
Coleman Goetz & Jack Stern

Ev - 'ry-bod - y's   ask - ing when___   We will be   at   peace a-gain,___   Ev - 'ry-
Ev - 'ry-one will   feel   so   gay,___   There'll be   one long   hol - i - day,___   When each

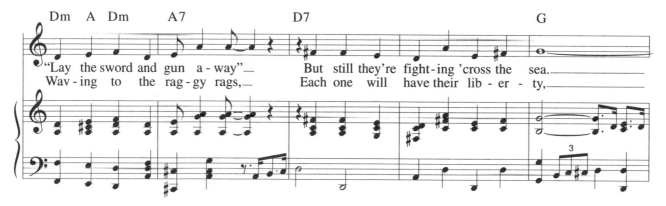

We're Going to Celebrate the End of the War in Ragtime

133

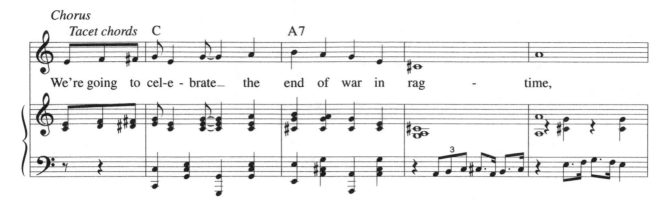

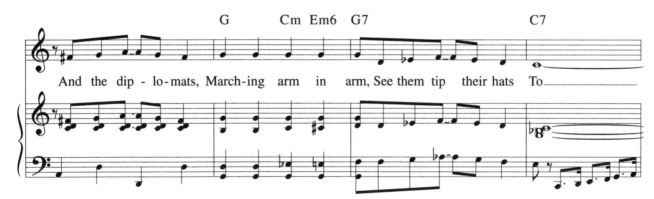

World War One

We Did It Before and We Can Do It Again

It didn't take long after the bombing of Pearl Harbor on December 7, 1941, for Cliff Friend and Charlie Tobias to come up with this bouncy, optimistic number. That fateful year, all America had been singing along with a sentimental British song, "There'll Be Bluebirds Over the White Cliffs of Dover." The Battle of Britain had been raging across the ocean, but now, far across another ocean, we were in it as well. By the following year, America's songwriters had gotten the message and responded with songs such as "Don't Get Around Much Anymore," "Don't Sit Under the Apple Tree with Anyone Else But Me," "I Left My Heart at the Stage-Door Canteen," "Praise the Lord and Pass the Ammunition," and "This Is the Army, Mister Jones." But "We Did It Before and We Can Do It Again" was the first.

We Did It Before and We Can Do It Again

Words and Music by
Cliff Friend & Charlie Tobias

December seventh, nineteen hundred and forty one _____ our land of freedom was defied; December eighth, nineteen hundred and forty one

©1941 WARNER BROS. INC
Copyright renewed and assigned to WARNER BROS. INC and CHED MUSIC

World War Two

140

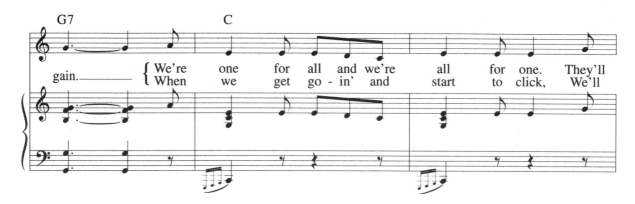

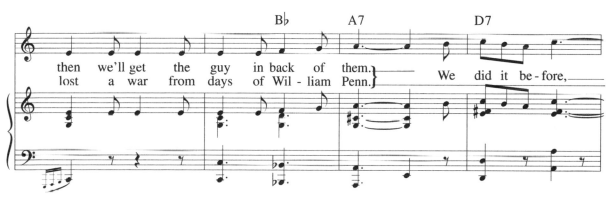

'Round and Around
Hitler's Grave

'Round and around Old Joe Clark,
'Round and around I say.
He'd follow me ten thousand miles
To hear my banjo play.

This fiddlers' and banjo pickers' favorite was a perfect medium for an endless stream of verses poking fun at Hitler *et al.* In Norman Corwin's 1945 radio drama *On a Note of Triumph,* this song was sung variously in Serbian (*Obil osimo okolo nokolo Hitlerovog groba, okolo nokolo*), Danish (*Og saa rundt om Hitler's grav, Hitler's grav, Hitler's grav*), and Greek (*Gyro sto mnima too Hitler gyro gyro pername*).

'Round and Around Hitler's Grave

The Ger-man ar - my gen-e-ral staff, They must have missed con -

nec-tions. They drove a hun-dred miles a day, But in the wrong di -

rec-tion. 'Round and a-round Hit-ler's grave, 'Round and a-round we

go.   We're gon-na   lay that   poor boy down,   He won't get up no more.

I wish I had a bushel,
I wish I had a peck,
I wish I had old Hitler
With a rope around his neck. *Chorus*

Hitler went to Russia
In search of Russian oil.
The only oil that he found
Was the oil in which he boiled. *Chorus*

They marched right into Russia,
Just like Napoleon.
But when the snows began to fall,
They knew their time had come. *Chorus*

I'm a-going overseas,
Tell you what I'll do,
I'll grab old Hitler by the neck,
And break it right in two. *Chorus*

Hitler he bombed London,
It was a mighty blitz;
But after we get through with him,
We'll give that poor boy fits. *Chorus*

Hitler said to Goering,
"We're in an awful fix,
The Yanks are dropping ten-ton bombs -
Berlin's a pile of bricks." *Chorus*

Hitler said the Third Reich
Would last a thousand years.
His tanks are rolling backwards now -
We've made him strip his gears. *Chorus*

If anyone should ask you,
Who was it sang this song,
It was a G. I. soldier boy,
As he does march along. *Chorus*

United Nations Make a Chain

Mary wore three links of chain,
Every link was Jesus' name,
Keep your hand on the plow, hold on.
Hold on, hold on,
Keep your hand on the plow, hold on.

At the end of World War Two, this inspirational Negro spiritual served as the basis of a song of hope for a peaceful future. We're still hoping.

United Nations Make a Chain

U - nit - ed   Na - tions make   a   chain,   Ev - 'ry   link   is   free - dom's

name.   Keep your   hand   on the   plough,   hold___   on.___

Hold   on,_____   hold   on._____   Keep your

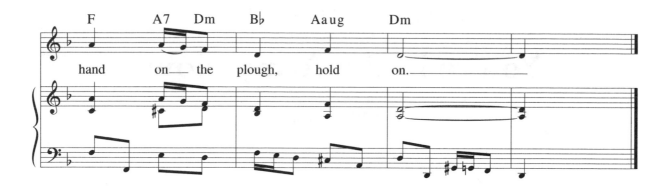

hand on the plough, hold on.

Now the war is over and done,
Let's keep the peace that we have won.
    Keep your hand on that plow, hold on! *Chorus*

Freedom's name is mighty sweet;
Black and white are gonna meet.
    Keep your hand on that plow, hold on! *Chorus*

Many men have fought and died
So we could be here side by side,
    Keep your hand on that plow, hold on! *Chorus*

You're in the Army Now

This sarcastic morale-booster of indeterminate origin was picked up and sung with pride by GIs on all army bases and on battlefields around the globe.

You're in the Army Now

America
(My Country 'Tis of Thee)

Just as a British melody supplied the tune for "The Star Spangled Banner," a German patriotic hymn, *"Gott Segne Unser Sachsenland"* ("God Bless Our Native Land"), inspired the creation of "America"—also known by its first line of "My Country 'Tis of Thee." Andover seminary student Samuel Francis Smith came across the German hymn while translating German poetry in 1832. He was struck by the German hymn's patriotic sentiments and felt that the United States also needed a stirring national poem. Within thirty minutes, he had completed the work, which he titled "America."

Fittingly, on July 4, 1832, the children's choir of Park Street Congregational Church in Boston sang "America" at a Sunday school celebration. The song's immediate acceptance was due as much to its patriotic sentiment as to its well-known tune—a surefire formula for success. The song remained moderately well known until the Civil War, when, swept up in the general patriotic fervor of the time, it took the North by storm.

The tune to "America" is the official or semiofficial melody of about twenty nations. For more than a century, the tune had been used for England's anthem, "God Save the King (or Queen)." As early as the seventeenth century, it could be found in Swiss music, and it had a long history of usage in Germany, Sweden, and Russia. Nine years after Smith adopted the melody, Beethoven wrote piano variations on it.

America
(My Country 'Tis of Thee)

Words by Samuel Francis Smith

Tune: " God Save the King"

My coun - try 'tis of thee, Sweet land of li - ber - ty,

Of thee I sing. Land where my fa - thers died!

Land of the pil - grim's pride! From ev - 'ry——

moun - tain - side Let____ free - dom ring

My Native country, Thee,
Land of the Noble free,
Thy name I love;
I love Thy rocks and rills.
Thy woods and templed hills
My heart with rapture thrills,
Like that above.

Let music swell the breeze,
And ring from all the trees
Sweet Freedom's song;
Let mortal tongues awake,
Let all that breathe partake,
Let rocks their silence break,
The sound prolong.

Our father's God! to Thee,
Author of Liberty,
To thee we sing;
Long may our land be bright
With freedom's holy light;
Protect us by Thy might,
Great God, our King!

America the Beautiful

Katharine Lee Bates, an English teacher at Wellesley College, wrote the original version of "America the Beautiful" in 1893. She wrote the second version in 1904. She penned her final version in 1913.

One day some of the other teachers and I decided to go on a trip to 14,000-foot Pikes Peak. We hired a prairie wagon. Near the top we had to leave the wagon and go the rest of the way on mules. I was very tired. But when I saw the view, I felt great joy. All the wonder of America seemed displayed there, with the sea-like expanse.

Soon after the original poem was published in 1895, it was set to various tunes. By the 1920s, it had become permanently joined with the tune "Materna," which Samuel Augustus Ward had composed in 1892 for the hymn "O Mother Dear, Jerusalem."

America the Beautiful

Words by Katherine Lee Bates

Music by Samuel A. Ward

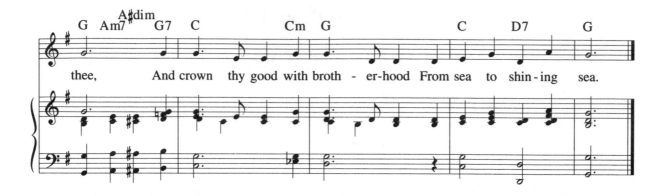

thee, And crown thy good with broth - er-hood From sea to shin-ing sea.

O beautiful for pilgrim feet whose stern impassion'd stress
A thouroughfare for freedom built across the wilderness.
America! America! God mend thy every flaw,
Confirm thy soul in self-control, thy liberty in law.

O beautiful for heroes prov'd in liberating strife,
Who more than self their country loved, and mercy more than life.
America! America! May God thy gold refine,
Till all success be nobleness, and every gain divine.

O beautiful for patriot dream that sees beyond the years
Thine alabaster cities gleam, undimmed by human tears.
America! America! God shed his grace on thee,
And crown thy good with brotherhood from sea to shining sea.

O beautiful for halcyon skies, for amber waves of grain,
For purple mountain majesties above the enameled plain!
America! America! God shed his grace on thee
Till souls wax fair as earth and air and music-hearted sea!

O beautiful for glory-tale of liberating strife
When once and twice, for man's avail men lavished precious life!
America! America! God shed his grace on thee
Till selfish gain no longer stain the banner of the free!

Anchors Aweigh

Originally composed in November 1906 as a Naval Academy football fight song, "Anchors Aweigh" was first sung at the Army-Navy game later that month. (Navy won for the first time in several seasons.) The song was adopted as the official song of the U.S. Navy in 1907.

In 1906, Midshipman First Class Alfred Miles had approached Lieutenant Charles A. Zimmerman, bandmaster of the Naval Academy Band since 1887, with a request to compose "a piece of music that would be inspiring . . . that would live forever." Miles then wrote the first two stanzas of the football song. Subsequently, George D. Lottman revised some of the original lyrics, making the song more than "merely" a football song. It is this revised version that is presented here first.

Anchors Aweigh

Words by George D. Lottman

Music by Lieut. Charles A. Zimmerman

Stand Navy out to sea,
Fight our battle cry.
We'll never change our course,
So vicious foe steer shy-y-y-y.
Roll out the T. N. T.
Anchors aweigh.
Sail on to victory,
And sink their bones to Davy Jones, hooray.

Anchors Aweigh

Midshipman (subsequently Captain) Miles's original lyrics.

Stand, Navy, down the field,
Sails set to the sky.
We'll never change our course,
So Army you steer shy-y-y-y.
Roll up the score, Navy,
Anchors aweigh,
Sail, Navy down the field
And sink the Army, sink the Army Grey.

Get underway, Navy,
Decks cleared for the fray.
We'll hoist true Navy Blue,
So Army, down your Grey-y-y-y.
Full speed ahead, Navy,
Army, heave to.
Furl Black and Grey and Gold
And hoist the Navy, hoist the Navy Blue.

Blue of the Seven Seas;
Gold of God's great sun;
Let these our colors be
Till all of time be done-n-n-n.
By Seven shore we learn
Navy's stern call:
Faith, courage, service true,
With honor over, honor over all.

America Song
(Love Song for Far-Off America)

There are countless songs about leaving the "old country" and coming to America. Some of the songs express nostalgic feelings about saying goodbye to friends and family. Others are full of excitement and anticipation about the wonders of America, real and imagined.

Crossing over the salty waves from Sweden to America by sail took more than three months in the early nineteenth century. When steamships came into service in the 1860s, the travel time was cut to less than one month. By the 1880s, the all-steam liners regularly cut the time to less than three weeks. When direct traffic was inaugurated from Gothenburg to New York in 1915, thirteen days was the average crossing time. All this to get to the "pretty girls," "roasted geese," and "cellars bursting with champagne."

America Song
(Love Song for Far-Off America)

English translation by Jerry Silverman

We must cross the salt - y waves, Broth - ers, get in mo - tion, And we'll reach A - me - ri - ca, Far a - cross the o - cean. How can such a

Chorus

thing be so? Ah well, it real - ly is, you know!

Too bad that A - me - ri - ca, Too bad that A -

mer 'ca lies so ve - ry far a - way!

Sweet as sugar are the trees,
Growing in the woods there.
Many are the pretty girls -
They are the real goods there. *Chorus*

If you wish for one of them,
Four or five do show up.
In the meadows and the fields,
Dollar bills do grow up. *Chorus*

Ducks and chickens fall like rain,
They are so enticing.
Roasted geese bring their own knives,
Ready for the slicing. *Chorus*

Cellars bursting with champagne,
Gaiety and song there.
Everyone's related,
And the sun shines all night long there. *Chorus*

America Song (Love Song for a Far-Off America)

'Round Her Neck She Wore a Yellow Ribbon

Dating from the mid-1830s, a song entitled "All Around My Hat"—"written by J. Ansell . . . composed and arranged by John Valentine . . . as sung by Jack Reeve with the most unbounded applause"—achieved a certain amount of popularity in the United States and England. When American soldiers began to sing the song toward the end of the nineteenth century, they adjusted the lyrics and, to some extent, the tune. The yellow ribbon, perhaps inspired by the yellow piping on the soldiers' blue uniforms, became a symbol of remembrance. It was this revised version of the song that was published in 1917 as American soldiers marched off to war in France.

Since then, the yellow ribbon has taken on an ever-widening meaning. It has become the symbol for the fight against certain diseases and for the campaign against drunken driving.

'Round Her Neck She Wore a Yellow Ribbon

'Round her neck she wore a yel-low rib-bon, She

wore it in the win-ter and the mer-ry month of May.

When they asked her why the de-co-ra-tion, She

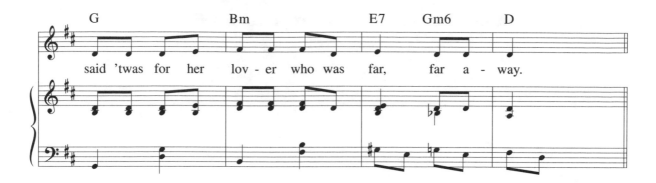

said 'twas for her lov-er who was far, far a-way.

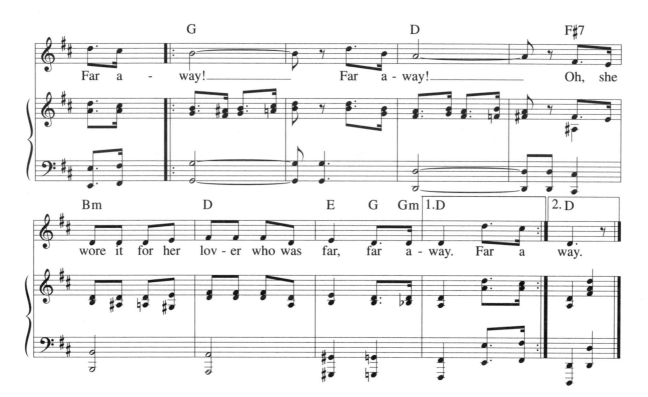

Far a-way!_____ Far a-way!_____ Oh, she

wore it for her lov-er who was far, far a-way. Far a way.

Above a grave she scattered yellow flowers,
She brought them in December and in the month of May.
And if you asked her why she came to bring them,
She said 'twas for a soldier who was six feet away.
    Far away! Far away!
    She brought them for a soldier who was six feet away.

The Caisson Song
(The Caissons Go Rolling Along)

Major Edmund L. Gruber was stationed in the Philippines in April 1908 when he was asked to write a song that would symbolize the spirit of the Fifth Field Artillery. In writing the song, he was inspired by an incident that occurred during a difficult march across the Zambales Mountains on the island of Luzon in 1907. At one point in the march, the main battalion became separated from the vanguard due to the rough terrain. A scout was sent to the top of a high peak to see if he could spot the missing battalion. In the distance, he heard the rumble of the gun carriages and the echoing shouts of the drivers as they urged their mule teams along.

The scout turned to (then) Lieutenant Gruber and said, "They'll be all right, Lieutenant, if they keep 'em rolling." As the battalion neared the point where Gruber was awaiting them, he heard the cry from the valley below: "Come on—keep 'em rolling!" The phrase stuck in his mind and he incorporated it into his song.

The Caisson Song
(The Caissons Go Rolling Along)

Words and Music by Major Edmund L. Gruber

O - ver hill, o - ver dale, we have hit the dust - y trail, And those cais - sons go rol - ling a - long. In and out, hear them shout: "Coun-ter march and right a -

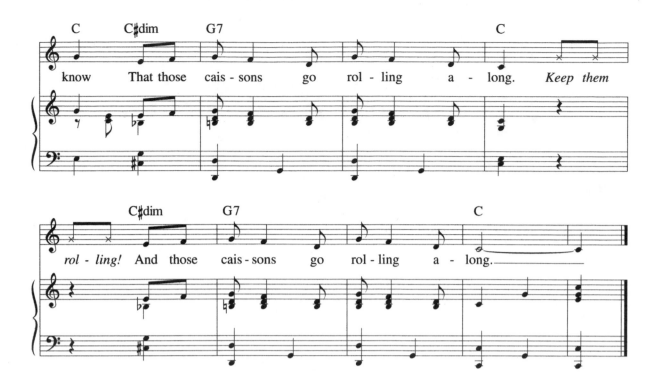

know That those cais-sons go rol-ling a-long. *Keep them*

rol-ling! And those cais-sons go rol-ling a-long._____

Through the storm, throught the night, up to where the doughboys [*or* GIs] fight,
All our caissons go rolling along.
At zero we'll be there, answering every call and flare,
While our caissons go rolling along. *Chorus*

Cavalry, boot to boot, we will join in the pursuit,
While those caissons go rolling along
Action front, at a trot: volley fire with shell and shot,
While those caissons go rolling along. *Chorus*

Should the foe penetrate, every gunner lies in wait,
And those caissons go rolling along.
Fire at will, lay 'em low, never stop for any foe,
While those caissons go rolling along. Chorus

But if fate me should call, and in action I should fall,
Keep those caissons a-rolling along.
Then in peace I'll abide, when I take my final ride
On a caisson that's rolling along. *Chorus*

Columbia, the Gem
of the Ocean

ritten in 1843 and extremely popular during the Lincoln years, "Columbia, the Gem of the Ocean" was usually included among the patriotic songs played by the Marine Band for the President's ceremonial gatherings.

Columbia, the Gem of the Ocean

Words and Music by David T. Shaw

O, Co - lum - bia! the gem of the ocean, The home of the brave— and the

free,_____ The shrine of each pa-triot's de - vo-tion A world— of-fers hom - age to

thee. Thy— man-dates make he - roes as - sem-ble When— Lib-er - ty's form— stands in

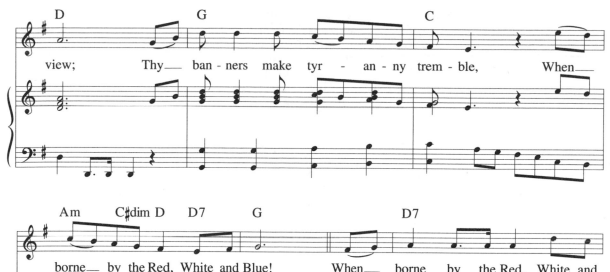

Columbia, the Gem of the Ocean

When the war winged its wide desolation,
And threatened the land to deform,
The ark then of freedom's foundation,
Columbia, rode safe through the storm:
With her garlands of vict'ry around her,
When so proudly she bore her brave crew,
With her flag proudly floating before her,
The boast of the Red, White, and Blue.
 The boast of the Red, White and Blue
 The boast of the Red, White and Blue,
 With her flag proudly floating before her,
 The boast of the Red, White and Blue.

The Union, the Union forever,
Our glorious nation's sweet hymn,
May the wreaths it has won never wither,
Nor the stars of its glory grow dim,
The wine cup, the wine cup bring hither,
And fill you it true to the brim!
May the wreaths they have won never wither,
Nor the star of their glory grow dim!
 The star-spangled banner bring hither,
 O'er Columbia's true sons let it wave;
 May the wreaths that have won never wither,
 Nor its stars cease to shine on the brave:

"Old Glory" to greet, now come hither,
With eyes full of love to the brim,
May the wreaths of the heroes ne'er wither,
Nor a star of our banner grow dim,
May the service, united, ne'er sever,
But they to their colours prove true;
The Army and Navy forever,
Three cheers for the Red, White and Blue.
 Three cheers for the Red, White and Blue
 Three cheers for the Red, White and Blue,
 The Army and Navy forever.
 Three cheers for the Red, White and Blue.

Hail, Columbia

T he author of the lyrics of this hymn was Joseph Hopkinson, son of Francis Hopkinson, one of the signers of the Declaration of Independence. Hopkinson adapted the music for the hymn in 1798 from "The President's March," which had been composed by Philip Phile in 1793. Hopkinson had this to say about the debut performance of "Hail *Columbia*":

It was written in the summer of 1798, when war with France was thought to be inevitable. Congress was then in session in this city [Philadelphia], deliberating upon that important subject, and acts of hostility had actually taken place. The contest between England and France was raging, and the people of the United States were divided into parties for the one side or the other; some thinking that policy and duty required us to espouse the cause of republican France, as she was called; others were for connecting ourselves with England, under the belief that she was the great preservative power of good principles and safe government . . . The theater was then open in our city. A young man belonging to it, whose talent was a singer . . . called on me on Saturday afternoon, his benefit being announced for the following Monday. His prospects were very disheartening; but he said that if he could get a patriotic song adapted to the tune of the "President's March," he did not doubt of a full house; that the poets of the theatrical corps had been trying to accomplish it, but had not succeeded. I told him that I would try what I could do for him. He came the next afternoon; and the song, such as it is, was ready for him. The object of the author was to get up an American spirit, which should be independent of, and above the interests of both belligerents: and look and feel exclusively for our own honor and rights. No allusion is made to France or England, or the quarrel between them: or to the question, which was most at fault in their treatment of us. Of course, the song found favor with both parties, for both were Americans; at least neither could disavow the sentiments and feelings it inculcated. Such is the history of this song which has endured beyond the expectation of the author, as it is beyond any merit it can boast of, except that of being truly and exclusively patriotic in its sentiments and spirit.

Hail, Columbia

Words by Joseph Hopkinson

Music by Philip Phile

Hail, Co-lum - bia, hap - py land, Hail, ye he - roes, heav'n - born band! Who fought and bled in free - dom's cause, Who fought and bled in free - dom's cause! And when the storm of

war - was — gone, En - joyed — the peace — your val - or won. Let

in - de-pen-dence be - your — boast, Ev - er mind - ful

what it cost, Ev - er — grate - ful for — the — prize,

Let its al - tar reach the skies. Firm, u - nit - ed,

Chorus

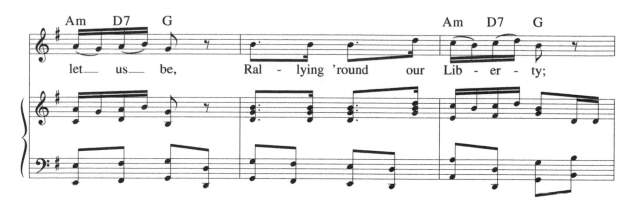

let___ us___ be, Ral - lying 'round our Lib - er - ty;

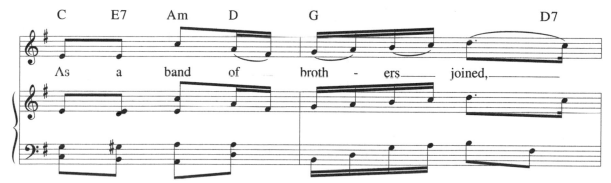

As a band of broth - ers___ joined,___

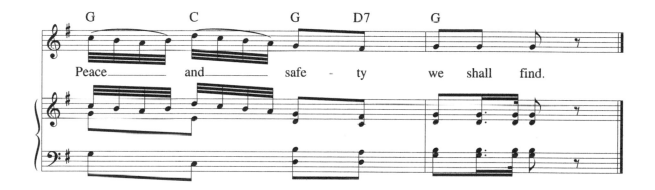

Peace___ and___ safe - ty we shall find.

Hail, Columbia

183

Immortal patriots, rise once more,
Defend your rights, defend your shore!
Let no rude foe with impious hand,
Let no rude foe with impious hand,
Invade the shrine where sacred lies
Of toil and blood, the well-earn'd prize.
While offering peace, sincere and just,
In heav'n we place a manly trust
That truth and justice will prevail,
And every scheme of bondage fail.   *Chorus*

Sound, sound the trump of fame,
Let Washington's great name
Ring through the world with loud applause,
Ring through the world with loud applause;
Let every clime to freedom dear
Listen with joyous ear;
With equal skill, with godlike pow'r.
He governs in the fearful hour
Of horrid war, or guides with ease
The happier times of honest peace.   *Chorus*

Behold the chief who now commands,
Once more to serve his country, stands,
The rock on which the storms will beat.
The rock on which the storms will beat;
His hopes are fixed on heaven and you.
When hope was sinking with dismay,
When glooms obscur'd Columbia's day,
His steady mind from changes free.
Resolv'd on death or liberty.   *Chorus*

Danish Flag and
Starry Banner

In 1871, Niels Pedersen (1848–1931) emigrated from Denmark to Racine, Wisconsin. He changed his name to Adam Dan, and it was under his new name that he wrote this hymn-like song in 1887. Dan was one of the founding fathers of the Danish Church in America and he edited its newspaper, *Kirkelig Samler* (*Church Chronicler*), in which the song was first published. The song is a pure expression of thanks (with a little critique thrown into the second and fifth verses) to America, but also gives a nod of acknowledgment to Denmark.

Danish Flag and Starry Banner

English translation by Jerry Silverman   **Words and Music by Adam Dan**

Dan - ish flag and Star - ry Ban-ner, You make quite a pair,

Here in the tall for - est man - or, In the sum - mer air.

Which flag has the great-er glo - ry? No one here can say. When it

comes to free-dom's sto - ry, Both have led the way. When it

comes to free-dom's sto - ry,_____ Both have led the way.

Real July Fourth memories
Are rarely given voice.
Speeches vanish with the breeze -
Tomfoolery and noise.
We, whose fathers crossed the ocean
In the good old days,
Shall as Danes, with great emotion,
Sing in freedom's praise.

Here are greater things in season
Than to have a farm.
Chopping wood's not the sole reason
That we raise our arm.
More than just to earn a living,
Shall we give our all.
Noble men, our freedom giving,
Built Liberty Hall.

We can make a contribution,
As we understand.
Strengthening the Constitution
Of this wond'rous land.
Washington fought here with bravery,
Franklin served us well,
And where Lincoln did crush slavery,
And where Garfield fell.

To July Fourth we give our thanks,
Day of Liberty.
No more silly, juvenile pranks -
Drinking noisily.
Danish Flag and Starry Banner,
We do you acclaim.
To this land we sing hosanna,
And from whence we came.

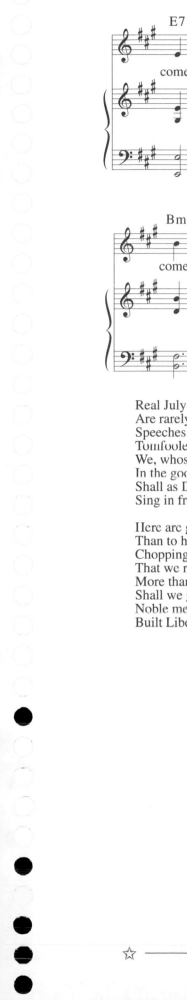

Danish Flag and Starry Banner

God Bless the U.S.A.

How do you measure the worth of a song? Many popular songs have brief lives before they fade from our memories as others take their place. When Lee Greenwood wrote "God Bless the U.S.A." in 1984, neither he nor anyone else could have imagined that 17 years later, the opening words of the song, "If tomorrow all the things were gone I'd worked for all my life," would take on such terrible meaning. When the Twin Towers of the World Trade Center crumbled on September 11, 2001, when the Pentagon was struck that very same unforgettable morning, it seemed to all of us that, indeed, "all the things were gone . . ." Yet, such is the power of an inspired song—and we have heard many others in our history—that we take comfort from its message of hope and hold our heads up a little higher as we sing it together.

God Bless the U. S. A.

Words and Music by Lee Greenwood

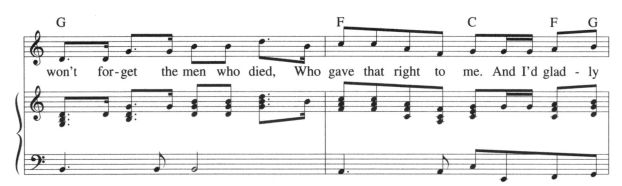

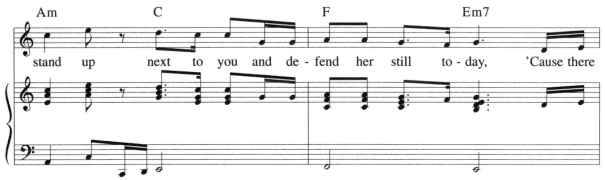

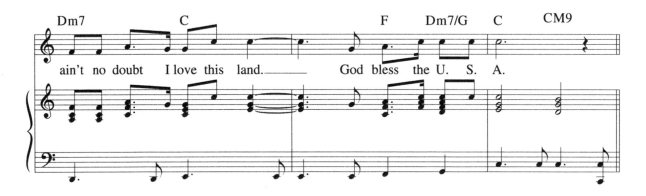

Americans All

Verse 2: From the lakes of Min - ne - so - ta to the

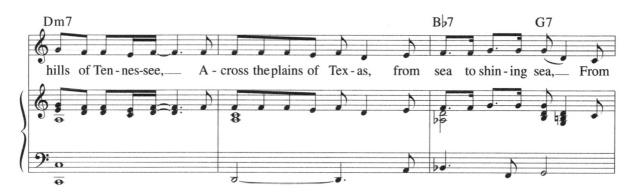

hills of Ten - nes-see,___ A - cross the plains of Tex - as, from sea to shin - ing sea,___ From

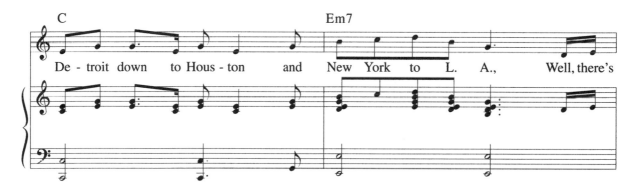

De - troit down to Hous - ton and New York to L. A., Well, there's

D.S. (Chorus) al Coda

pride in ev - 'ry A-mer - i - can heart, And it's time to stand and say___ That I'm

Coda   *Chorus*

— God bless the U. S. A.   And I'm proud to be an A-mer-i-can—where at

least I know I'm free,   And I won't for-get   the men who died,   who

gave that right to me. And I'd glad - ly stand   up   next   to you, and de-

fend her still to-day, 'Cause there ain't no doubt I love this land:— God bless the U. S. A.—

Americans All

Hail to the Chief

O n May 8, 1812, a performance of a stage version of Sir Walter Scott's epic poem "The Lady of the Lake" was given in New York City. Included in the performance was a musical setting by James Sanderson of a portion of canto two of the "Boat Song," entitled "Hail to the Chief." This musical setting had probably been composed in 1810, since Scott mentions in a letter to a friend in November of that year that he had received a copy of the song.

Shortly after its May performance in New York, "Hail to the Chief" was published in America; copies of that original music can be found today in the archives of the Military District of Washington. After being published, the song gained wide popularity as a march as well as a vehicle for political and patriotic parodies. Because of its martial character and the appropriateness of its title, it gradually transitioned from just a popular tune to a march that has enjoyed "official" status as the fanfare reserved exclusively for presidential appearances.

Hail to the Chief

Words by Thomas Ellis

Music by James Sanderson

Hail to the Chief_____ Of our be-lov - ed na - tion.

Hail to the Chief,_____ In whom we put our trust.

Hail to the Chief,_____ Our hope and in - spi - ra - tion.

Serv - ing the cause to pre - serve our lib - er - ty. With sin - cere de-

vo - tion we sup - port our great com - man - der, Know - ing in him we can

place our be - lief. May God al - ways guide him, and lead him on his

way. Hail to the pre - si - dent! Hail to the Chief!

Hail to the Chief

Home on the Range

Ever since 1785, the policy of the U.S. government had been to support the idea that the public domain (unsettled public land) belonged to the people and that every family was entitled to a home or farm. The initial result of this policy was that speculators bought up large tracts of land in the thirteen original states and then offered them for sale to those who could pay the price. This was not exactly what the government had had in mind. Poor immigrants could hardly afford to become landowners under these conditions.

As the frontier gradually pushed westward, some attempt was made to relieve this situation in 1841, when the government offered public-domain land for sale west of the Appalachians at $1.25 an acre. This was not the "free land" that many had hoped for, however, and over the next twenty years, a number of "homestead bills," designed to give some relief to prospective settlers, were introduced in Congress.

Then, on May 20, 1862—with the Civil War raging—President Lincoln signed into law the Homestead Act. It provided that any citizen or any alien who had declared his or her intention of becoming a citizen, on the payment of $10, could file a claim for up to 160 acres. A further stipulation was that the settler, after having "resided upon or cultivated" that land for the following five years, could receive permanent title to the land. But it wasn't always easy.

There were no forests on the plains—no trees to provide lumber for even the simplest log cabin, let alone for a farmhouse and barn. Even the building of fences posed problems. The "little old sod shanty on the plain" was often just a dugout with an earthen roof—a roof that dripped water for days after a rain. When it rained, that is. One worn-out farmer said: "In God we trusted, in Kansas we busted . . . what with sand storms, cyclones, dry weather, blizzards and grasshoppers."

Another homesteader put it this way: "I've got a little bet with the government. They're betting me I can't live here for five years, and I'm betting them that I can."

Some homesteaders lost the bet, but most won it.

Despite all the hardships, the loneliness, the uncertainties, and the backbreaking labor, the settlers' crops grew and their land prospered. The railroads, in whose best interest it was to see the land populated, spread their networks throughout the new territories. They printed glowing advertisements and posters that they hoped would entice families to move out west and start a new life on "Uncle Sam's farm." That the response was good to this "general invitation to the people of the world" was amply proven by the fact that during the forty-year period immediately following the Homestead Act, 718,930 homesteads containing 96,495,414 acres were established.

In 1873, a prairie doctor named Higley Brewster, whose medical office and home in Smith County, Kansas, were a typical dugout, looked about him and recognized the beauty of the land. He was so moved by his emotions that he wrote a poem, which, when set to music by Daniel E. Kelly, became the most famous of all the Western songs, "Home on the Range." The song was adopted as the official state song of Kansas in 1947.

Home on the Range

Lyrics by Higley Brewster

Music by Daniel E. Kelly

Oh, give me a home where the buf - fa - lo roam, Where the

deer and the an - te - lope play;_____ Where

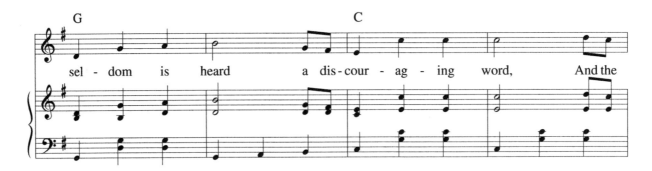

sel - dom is heard a dis - cour - ag - ing word, And the

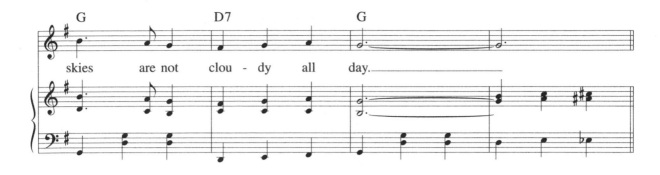

Home on the Range

Oh! Give me the land where the bright diamond sand
Throws its light from the glittering streams,
Where glideth along the graceful white swan,
Like the maid to her heavenly dreams.   *Chorus*

How often the night, when the heavens were bright,
With the light of the twinkling stars,
Have I stood there amazed, and asked as I gazed,
If their glory exceeds that of ours.   *Chorus*

I love the wild flowers in this bright land of ours,
I love the wild curlew's shrill scream;
The bluffs and the white rocks and antelope flocks,
That graze on the mountain so green.   *Chorus*

The air is so pure and the breezes so free,
The zephyrs so balmy and light,
That I would not exchange my home on the range
For all of the cities so bright.   *Chorus*

Leben Zoll Kolumbus
(Long Life to Columbus)

When it came to flag-waving, patriotic zeal, nothing surpassed the enthusiasm of the immigrants who arrived on our shores at the end of the nineteenth century and in the early years of the twentieth. These immigrants, escaping from poverty and oppression in Europe, found their joy over living in a free land nowhere better expressed than in this rousing number from the once-flourishing Yiddish-language theater that took root on Second Avenue in New York City. Christopher Columbus was an often-used symbol for the good and the bad encountered in America.

Leben Zoll Kolumbus
(Long Life to Columbus)

Words by A. Perlmutter
English translation by Jerry Silverman

Music by H. Wohl

A shte - tl iz A - me - ri - ke,
A - mer - i - ca's a hap - py place,

A me - khay - e khle - bn; Es rut oyf ir di shkhi - ne - le, Mir
Real - ly, what a treas - ure. You'll see it plain on ev - 'ry face, There's

zol - n a - zoy le - bn. Mil - kho - mes, bik - sn, men - tshn blut
noth - ing here but plea - sure. For wars and guns and shed - ding blood,

Leben Zoll Kolumbus (*Long Life to Columbus*)

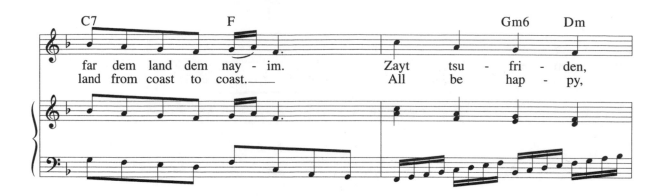

far dem land dem nay - im.   Zayt tsu - fri - den,
land from coast to coast.____   All be hap - py,

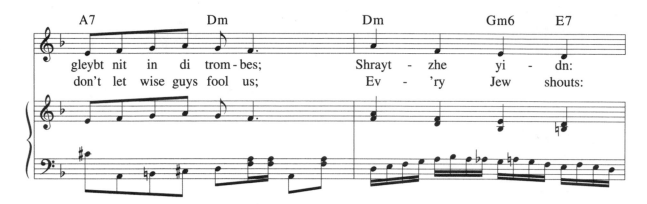

gleybt nit in di trom - bes;   Shrayt - zhe yi - dn:
don't let wise guys fool us;   Ev - 'ry Jew shouts:

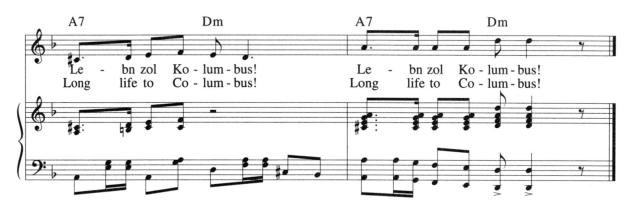

Le - bn zol Ko - lum - bus!   Le - bn zol Ko - lum - bus!
Long life to Co - lum - bus!   Long life to Co - lum - bus!

Americans All

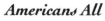

204

I'm on My Way to the
Freedom Land

The great Civil Rights Movement of the 1960s was inspired to a large extent by songs. Often drawn from the rich tradition of Negro spirituals, these songs expressed a true sense of patriotism: the desire of all Americans to participate in, and benefit from, the American dream.

I'm on My Way to the Freedom Land

I'm on my way⎯ to the free - dom land.⎯

⎯ I'm on my way⎯ to the free - dom land.⎯

⎯ I'm on my way⎯ to the free - dom land.⎯

I'll ask my brother to come with me.
I'll ask my brother to come with me.
I'll ask my brother to come with me.
I'm on my way, Great God, I'm on my way.

If he can't go, I'll go anyhow.
If he can't go, I'll go anyhow.
If he can't go, I'll go anyhow.
I'm on my way, Great God, I'm on my way.

I'll ask my sister to come with me.
I'll ask my sister to come with me.
I'll ask my sister to come with me.
I'm on my way, Great God, I'm on my way.

If you can't go, don't hinder me.
If you can't go, don't hinder me.
If you can't go, don't hinder me.
I'm on my way, Great God, I'm on my way.

If you can't go, let your children go.
If you can't go, let your children go.
If you can't go, let your children go.
I'm on my way, Great God, I'm on my way.

Repeat verse one.

I'm on My Way to the Freedom Land

The House I Live In

This song was the inspiration for the 1945 Academy Award–winning short film of the same name featuring Frank Sinatra. Sinatra also recorded the song that same year. Another memorable recording of the song was made by Paul Robeson.

Lewis Allen is remembered for his powerful anti-lynching song "Strange Fruit," which was sung and recorded by Billie Holiday and Josh White. Earl Robinson was a prolific composer of Americana songs, including "Joe Hill," "The Ballad for Americans," and "The Lonesome Train" (a cantata describing the voyage of Abraham Lincoln's funeral train).

When singing "The House I Live In," we can bring the lyrics in measures 35 and 36 up to date with a slight change: "The dream that's been a-growin' for more than two hundred years."

The House I Live In

Words by Lewis Allen

Music by Earl Robinson

Americans All

The House I Live In

hun-dred fif-ty years.　The town I live in,　the street, the house, the room,　The

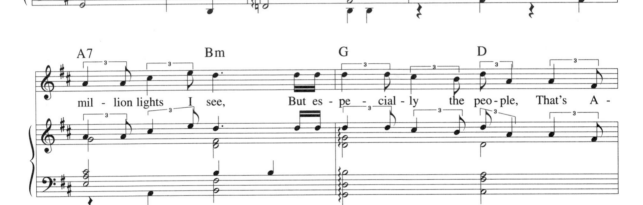

pave-ment of the cit-y, or a　gar-den all in bloom, The church, the school, the club-house, The

mil-lion lights I see,　But es-pe-cial-ly　the peo-ple, That's A-

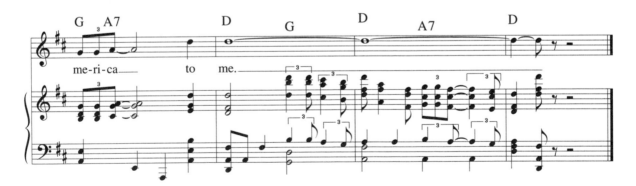

me-ri-ca　　to me.

Jefferson and Liberty

Robert Treat Paine, Jr., had composed a song in 1798 entitled "Adams and Liberty," but that didn't prevent him from penning this ode to Thomas Jefferson some three years later. "Jefferson and Liberty" was first performed on March 11, 1801, in Wallingford, Connecticut, in celebration of Jefferson's election. The tune Paine had chosen for "Adams and Liberty" was "To Anacreon in Heaven," which, as we have seen, now carries the lyrics of "The Star Spangled Banner." For "Jefferson and Liberty," he chose the more sprightly Irish reel "Gobby-O."

Adams and his fellow Federalists had identified more with the "respectable" politics of Great Britain (erstwhile foe) than with the "anarchistic" tendencies of the French (erstwhile ally). Jefferson and his fellow Republicans did not trust the British and instead identified with the populist ideals of the French Revolution. The Federalists, who were in control of Congress in 1798, passed laws, modeled after repressive British laws, that raised the number of years necessary for naturalization from five to fourteen, permitted the president to arrest or deport any alien whom he considered a threat to the country, and permitted the arrest or deportation of any subject of a foreign power with whom the United States might be at war. Taken together, these laws were dubbed the Alien and Sedition Laws. They had a chilling effect on free speech because, for example, many newspaper editors were both Republicans and aliens.

Thus, the "reign of terror" mentioned in the first verse of "Jefferson and Liberty" had made serious inroads on the Bill of Rights with its arrests of newspaper editors and a general atmosphere of political repression. The Alien and Sedition Laws, as can be imagined, were extremely unpopular and were swept away after Jefferson's election to the presidency in 1800.

Jefferson and Liberty

Words and Music by Robert Treat Paine

The gloom-y night be-fore us flies, The reign of ter - ror
is no more; Its gags, in-quis - i - tors and spies, Its herds of har - pies
are no more. Re - joice, Co-lum - bia's sons, re-joice, To ty - rants nev - er

bend___ the knee; But join with heart and soul___ and voice, For___ Jef - fer - son___ and li - ber - ty.

O'er vast Columbia's varied clime,
Her cities, forests, shores and dales,
In rising majesty sublime,
Immortal Liberty prevails. *Chorus*

Hail, long expected, glorious day!
Illustrious, memorable morn,
That Freedom's fabric from decay
Rebuilds, for millions yet unborn. *Chorus*

His country's surest hope and stay,
In virtue and in talents tried,
Now rises to assure the sway,
O'er Freedom's Temple to provide. *Chorus*

Within its hallowed walls immense,
No hireling Bands shall e'er arise,
Arrayed in Tyranny's defense,
To crush an injured people's cries. *Chorus*

No Lordling here with gorging jaws,
Shall wring from Industry its food;
Nor fiery bigot's Holy Laws
Lay waste our fields and streets in blood. *Chorus*

Here Strangers from a thousand shores,
Compelled by Tyranny to roam,
Shall find among abundant stores,
A nobler and a happier home. *Chorus*

Here Art shall lift her laureled head,
Wealth, Industry and Peace divine,
And where dark pathless Forests spread,
Rich fields and lofty cities shine. *Chorus*

From Europe's wants and woes remote,
A dreary waste of waves between,
Here plenty cheers the humblest cot,
And smiles on every Village Green. *Chorus*

Here, free as air's expanded space,
To every soul and sect shall be
The sacred priv'lege of our race,
The Worship of the Deity. *Chorus*

These gifts, great Liberty, are thine;
Ten thousand more we owe to thee -
Immortal may their mem'ries shine
Who fought and died for Liberty. *Chorus*

What heart but hails a scene so bright,
What soul but inspiration draws,
Who would not guard so dear a right,
Or die in such a glorious cause? *Chorus*

Let Foes to Freedom dread the name,
But should they touch the sacred Tree,
Twice fifty thousand swords shall flame
For Jefferson and Liberty. *Chorus*

From Georgia to Lake Champlain,
From seas to Mississippi's shore,
The Sons of Freedom loud proclaim,
The Reign of Terror now is o'er. *Chorus*

Jefferson and Liberty

The Marines' Hymn

After the Marines took part in the capture of Derna (Darnah), in what is now Libya, during the war with the Barbary Pirates in 1805, the Colors of the Corps were inscribed with the words: "To the Shores of Tripoli." When in 1847, the Marines participated in the capture and occupation of Mexico City and the Castle of Chapultepec, otherwise known as the Halls of Montezuma, the inscription was expanded to: "From the Shores of Tripoli to the Halls of Montezuma." It was following this campaign that, according to tradition, a Marine on duty in Mexico City, while composing what would eventually become the first verse of the hymn, felt that the line did not "scan" well and transposed the phrase to the now familiar: "From the halls of Montezuma to the shores of Tripoli." The tune to which the words are set is derived from an aria found in the opera "Genevieve de Brabant," composed by Jacques Offenbach and first presented in Paris on November 19, 1859.

The Marines' Hymn

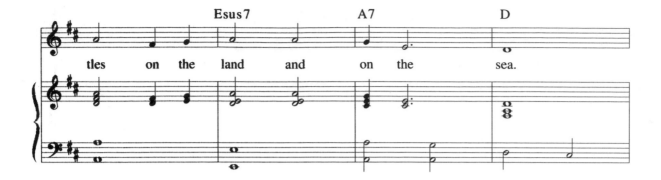

tles on the land and on the sea.

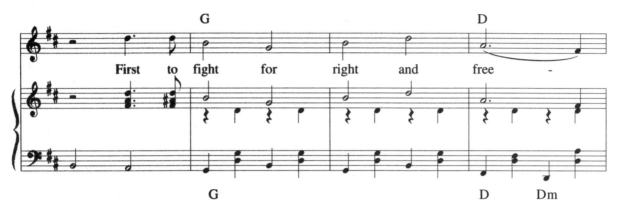

First to fight for right and free - dom,

and to keep our hon - or clean,

We are proud to bear the ti -

Americans All

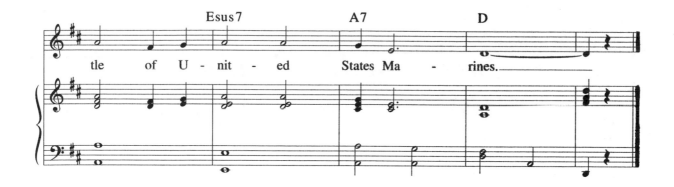

tle of U - nit - ed States Ma - rines.

Our flag's unfurled to every breeze from dawn to setting sun;
We have fought in every clime and place where we could take a gun;
In the snow of far-off northern lands and in sunny tropic scenes;
You will always find us on the job, the United States Marines.

Here's a health to you and to our corps, which we are proud to serve;
In many a strife we've fought for life, and never lost our nerve.
If the Army and the Navy ever looked on heaven's scenes,
They would find the streets are guarded by United States Marines.

The Marines' Hymn

Lied vom Mississippi
(Mississippi Song)

Only the German text of this enthusiastic song has come down to us, accompanied by the vague indication: "1844—*Nach einer Negermelodie*" (to a Negro melody). The melody, "The Patriotic Diggers," written by Samuel Woodward during the War of 1812, although not a "Negro melody," seems to fit perfectly with the rhythmic bounce of the text.

Lied vom Mississippi
(Mississippi Song)

English translation by Jerry Silverman **Music: "The Patriotic Diggers"**

Brü - der · laßt uns froh   Jetzt das Glas er -
Bro - thers, in our joy   Let us lift our

he - ben, ·   Denn wir kön - nen frei
glas - ses,   For we're liv - ing here,

Nur im Aus - land le - ben.   Kön - nen oh - ne
And we need no pas - ses.   In this for - eign

Lied vom Mississippi *(Mississippi Song)*

Freies Denken gilt
So wie freies Sprechen.
Nirgend, nirgerd hier
Für ein Staatsverbrechen.
Hier macht kein Gendarme
Jemals uns Bedrängnis,
Und kein Bettlevogt
Führt uns in Gefängnis -
  Hier am Mississippi.

Adel, Ordenskram,
Titel, Räng und Stände,
Und zolch dummes Zeug,
Hat allhie ein Ende.
Hier darf nie ein Pfaff
Mit der Höll uns plagen.
Nie ein Jesuit
Uns die Ruh verjagen -
  Hier am Mississippi.

Früher lebten wir
Gleichsam nur zur Strafe,
Und man schor auch uns
Eben wie die Schafe.
Brüder, laßt uns drum
Singen, trinkcn, tanzen!
Keiner darf und kann
Hier uns je kuranzen -
  Hier am Mississippi.

Michel, baue nicht,
Ferner deine Saaten
Fürs Beamtenheer
Und die Herrn Soldatcn!
Michel, faß ein Herz,
Endlich auszuwandcrn:
Hier gehörst du dir,
Dort nur stets den andern -
  Hier am Mississippi.

Our thoughts are free,
Freedom of expression.
Nowhere, nowhere here
Political repression.
Here there's no *gendarme*
That will give us trouble.
Here no beadle leads us
To prison on the double -
  On the Mississippi.

Nobles, medal-junk,
Title, rank and standing,
And such stupid stuff,
Here does find an ending.
Here there are no priests
Threatening to curb us,
And no Jesuits
Are here to disturb us -
  On the Mississippi.

Formerly we lived
Lives of constant fearing,
And we were like sheep
Led unto the shearing.
Brothers, let us go
Where our fortunes land us.
Singing, drinking, dancing,
None to reprimand us -
  On the Mississippi.

Michael, do not sow
Your seeds anymore now
For the bureaucrats
And the men of war now.
Michael, listen here -
Leave with all your brothers.
Here you're your own man,
There you are another's -
  On the Mississippi.

Lied vom Mississippi (*Mississippi Song*)

The New Colossus

This poem by New York–born poet Emma Lazarus (1849–1887) is inscribed on a tablet at the base of the Statue of Liberty. Emma Lazarus was a member of the oldest Jewish congregation in New York. The Russian pogroms of 1880 and 1881, which sent so many terrified Jews fleeing to America, were a trumpet call to her. Many of her poems reflect her reaction to those tragic events. Although "The New Colossus" was inspired by a specific series of tragic events, it speaks now to all humanity.

The New Colossus

Words by Emma Lazarus

Music by Jerry Silverman

The New Colossus

Americans All

The New Colossus

The Stars and Stripes Forever

In late 1896, while on vacation in Italy with his wife, John Philip Sousa received word that the manager of the Sousa Band, David Blakely, had suddenly died. The band was scheduled to begin another American cross-country tour soon, and Sousa knew he must return at once to take over the band's business affairs. Sousa tells the rest of the story in his autobiography, *Marching Along:*

> Here came one of the most vivid incidents of my career. As the vessel [the *Teutonic*] steamed out of the harbor I was pacing on the deck, absorbed in thoughts of my manager's death and the many duties and decisions which awaited me in New York. Suddenly, I began to sense a rhythmic beat of a band playing within my brain. Throughout the whole tense voyage, that imaginary band continued to unfold the same themes, echoing and re-echoing the most distinct melody. I did not transfer a note of that music to paper while I was on the steamer, but when we reached shore, I set down the measures that my brain-band had been playing for me, and not a note of it has ever changed.

The march was an immediate success, and Sousa's Band played it at almost every concert until his death more than twenty-five years later.

The Stars and Stripes Forever

Words and Music by John Philip Sousa

Let
Let

mar – tial note   In tri – umph float,   And lib – er – ty ex – tend   its might – y hand. A
ea – gle shriek. From lof – ty peak,   The nev – er – end – ing watch-word of our land. Let

flag   ap – pears 'Mid thun – d'rous cheers, The ban-ner of the west – ern land.   The
sum – mer breeze waft through the trees;   The ech – o of the cho – rus grand.   Sing

em – blem of   the brave   and true,   Its   folds   pro-tect   no   ty – rant crew, The
out   for lib – er – ty   and light, Sing   out   for free – dom   and   the right. Sing

The Stars and Stripes Forever

229

red   and white   and star - ry blue, Is   free - dom's shield   and   hope.
out   for Un - ion and   its might, Oh,   pa - tri - o - tic   Sons!

Oth - er   na - tions may deem   their   flags   the   best,   And___

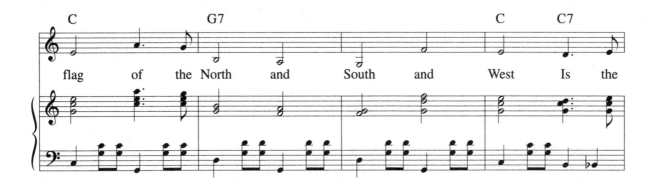

cheer them   with   fer - vid   e - la - tion.   But   the

flag   of   the North   and   South   and   West   Is   the

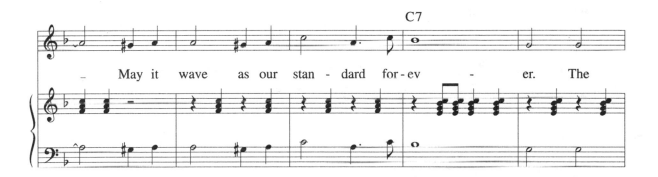

The Stars and Stripes Forever

of the Right._____ Let des - pots re - mem - ber the

day_____ When our fa - thers with might - y en-deav -

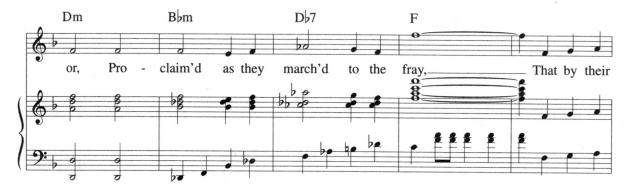

or, Pro - claim'd as they march'd to the fray,_____ That by their

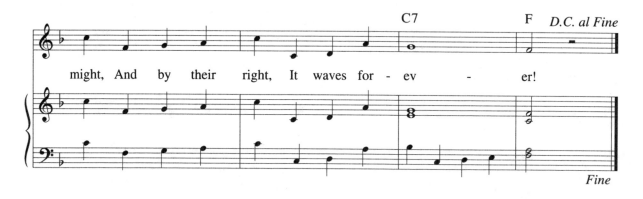

might, And by their right, It waves for - ev - er!

D.C. al Fine

Fine

The Pledge of Allegiance

"The Pledge of Allegiance" has undergone several modifications since it was first introduced on September 8, 1892, in the pages of the Boston-based magazine *The Youth's Companion*. Under the title "The Pledge to the Flag," the composition was the earliest version of what we now know as "The Pledge of Allegiance." It was designed to be used by schoolchildren during the activities the following month to commemorate the four-hundredth anniversary of Columbus's discovery of America. The October 11, 1892, Columbus Day celebration had been planned for years in advance, and this "pledge" was intended to sum up the feelings of patriotism and gratitude to this nation that were to be the touchstone of the celebration.

Two men interested both in education and in the planned Columbus Day celebrations in our nation's forty-four states were Francis Bellamy and James Upham. James Upham, an employee of the Boston publishing firm that produced *The Youth's Companion*, in which the poem first appeared, and Francis Bellamy, an educator who served as chairman of the National Committee of Educators and Civic Leaders, were involved in organizing the Columbus Day activities in Boston. Although Bellamy has been given credit for composing the words that were to become "The Pledge of Allegiance," for many years the actual authorship of "The Pledge" was in doubt, since the piece had been published anonymously and had never been copyrighted. What we do know for certain is that a month after its initial publication, its words were recited for the first time by more than 12 million schoolchildren across the nation. That first "Pledge of Allegiance" read:

> I pledge allegiance to my Flag, and to the Republic for which it stands: One Nation indivisible, with Liberty and Justice for all.

Over the coming years, some people began to feel that with all the new immigrants pouring into the country, some confusion might arise over the exact meaning of the words "my Flag." Therefore, in 1923, the text was altered to leave no doubt:

I pledge allegiance to the Flag of the United States of America, and to the Republic for which it stands: One Nation indivisible, with Liberty and Justice for all.

"The Pledge" took on added significance during the patriotic fervor created by World War Two. However, it remained an "unofficial" pledge until June 22, 1942, when the U.S. Congress included "The Pledge to the Flag" in the U.S. Flag Code. This was the first official sanction given to the words that had been recited each day by American children for almost fifty years. One year after this official sanction, the U.S. Supreme Court ruled that schoolchildren could not be forced to recite "The Pledge" as part of their daily scholastic routines. In 1945, "The Pledge to the Flag" received its official title of "The Pledge of Allegiance."

The final change to "The Pledge of Allegiance" occurred on June 14 (Flag Day), 1954, when President Dwight D. Eisenhower approved adding the words "under God." As he authorized this change, he said: "In this way we are reaffirming the transcendence of religious faith in America's heritage and future; in this way we shall constantly strengthen those spiritual weapons which forever will be our country's most powerful resource in peace and war."

The Pledge of Allegiance

Words by Francis Bellamy

Music by Jerry Silverman

Semper Paratus
(Always Ready)

One day during the winter of 1922 the inspiration came to me to write a song of the Coast Guard. It was one of those so-called "flashes" that come to people . . . and so I went below to my cabin on the *Yamacraw* and wrote the words to the song which I named "Semper Paratus" . . . it was not until the summer of 1926 while on shore duty at Unalaska, Bering Sea, that the air came to me while seated at the piano in the Company House. I tinkered over the air a few times and then called our dental surgeon, an accomplished violinist, for his opinion. It was commendatory . . . I told him that I could visualize and hear the march being played by a military band in full throat as a stirring march, or syncopated by an orchestra as a fox trot [!] . . . Last winter the Norfolk Unit of the League of Coast Guard Women gave a very wonderful dance at the Ghent Club. They played "Semper Paratus" arranged for a nine-piece orchestra. It was wonderfully received and received encore after encore.

—Captain Van, in a letter to the editor of *The Coast Guard*, October 24, 1927

Semper Paratus
(Always Ready)

Words and Music by Captain Francis Van Boskerck, USCG

From Az - tec shore to Arc-tic zone, To Eu - rope and Far

East, The flag is car - ried by our ships In times of war and

peace. And nev - er have we struck it yet, In

spite of foe-men's might, Who cheered our crews and cheered a-gain,___ For show - ing how to fight.

Chorus
So here's the Coast Guard marching song,
We sing on land and sea.
Through surf and storm and howling gale,
High shall our purpose be.
"Semper Paratus" is our guide,
Our fame and glory too.
To fight to save or fight to die,
Aye! Coast Guard we are for you.

Surveyor and *Narcissus,*
The *Eagle* and *Dispatch,*
The *Hudson* and the *Tampa* too,
The names are hard to match.
From Barrow's shores to Paraguay,
Great Lakes or ocean wave,
The Coast Guard fought through storms and winds,
To punish or to save. *Chorus*

Aye, we've been "Always Ready"
To do, to fight and die,
Write glory to the shield we wear
In letters to the sky.
To sink our foe or save the maimed,
Our mission and our pride
We'll carry on 'til Kingdom Come -
Ideals for which we've died. *Chorus*

Taps

Prior to the Civil War, the infantry used many different "bugle calls," which are melodies played on a bugle to communicate with often-distant troops. These calls included the wake-up call ("reveille"), meal call ("mess"), fall-in, charge, and call to extinguish lights ("lights out"). Since the earliest days, the bugle call for lights out, no matter what melody was used, has been called "Taps."

At the beginning of the Civil War, the Union Infantry's call to extinguish lights was the bugle-call melody from Silas Casey's book called "Tactics." In July 1862, General Daniel Butterfield ordered his troops to use a different call for lights out. The following history was provided by the bugler in the general's army brigade, Private Oliver Wilcox Norton, in a letter dated August 8, 1898:

> During the early part of the Civil War, I was bugler at the Headquarters of Butterfield's Brigade, Meroll's Division, Fitz-John Porter's Corp, Army of the Potomac. Up to July, 1862, the Infantry call for Taps was that set down in Casey's Tactics, which . . . was borrowed from the French. One day, soon after the seven days battles on the Peninsular, when the Army of the Potomac was lying in camp at Harrison's Landing, General Daniel Butterfield, then commanding our Brigade, sent for me, and showing me some notes on a staff written in pencil on the back of an envelope, asked me to sound them on my bugle. I did this several times, playing the music as written. He changed it somewhat, lengthening some notes and shortening others, but retaining the melody as he first gave it to me. After getting it to his satisfaction, he directed me to sound that call for Taps thereafter in place of the regulation call. The music was beautiful on that still summer night, and was heard far beyond the limits of our Brigade. The next day I was visited by several buglers from neighboring Brigades, asking for copies of the music which I gladly furnished. I think no general order was issued from army headquarters authorizing the substitution

of this for the regulation call, but as each brigade commander exercised his own discretion in such minor matters, the call was gradually taken up through the Army of the Potomac.

In a letter dated August 31, 1898, General Butterfield confirmed the essence of the bugler's story. Subsequent research has traced the origin of the original notes to a call known as "Scott's Tattoo," which had been used to signal troops to prepare their bedrolls one hour before lights out. General Butterfield altered a few notes and the tempo, but he kept the basic melody the same.

Beginning in July 1862, the twenty-four-note melody used as a call for lights out spread through the Union Army. However, the first time it was played for the burial of a soldier was during the Peninsular Campaign, later that year. A Union cannoneer had been killed in action, and his burial was being prepared. Military protocol at the time required that the Union soldier be honored with a traditional three-volley salute. However, the Union soldiers were concealed in the woods and the Confederate Army was close. The officer in charge, Captain John C. Tidball of Battery A, Second Artillery, feared that the traditional round of volleys would arouse the enemy. Therefore, Captain Tidball ordered instead that "Taps" be substituted for the gunfire. This first sounding of "Taps" at a military funeral is commemorated in a stained glass window at the Chapel of the Centurion (The Old Post Chapel) at Fort Monroe, Virginia. The window, made by R. Geissler of New York and based on a painting by Sidney King, was dedicated in 1958 and shows a bugler and a flag at half-staff. The earliest official reference to the mandatory use of "Taps" at military funeral ceremonies is found in the U.S. Army Infantry Drill Regulations for 1891.

Taps

Fad-ing light Dims the sight, And a star gems the sky, Gleam-ing

bright. From a-far, draw-ing nigh, Falls the night.

Dear one, rest!
In the west.
Sable night lulls the day on her breast.
Sweet, good night,
Now away
To thy rest.

Day is done,
Gone the sun
From the lakes, from the hills, from the sky.
All is well,
Safely rest,
God is nigh.

Then good night,
Peaceful night,
Till the light of the dawn shineth bright,
God is near,
Do not fear -
Friend, good night.

This Land Is Your Land

Woody Guthrie's simple, heartfelt ballad about the beauty of America first appeared in print in the Fall 1954 issue of the folk-song magazine *Sing Out*. At the time, I was editing the music for the magazine, and when Woody's song arrived at our office, we all felt that this was one destined to become one of the all-time great musical statements about our country. The song has more than fulfilled our expectations.

This Land Is Your Land

This Land Is Your Land

This land was made for you and me.

As I was walking that ribbon of highway,
I saw above me that endless skyway.
I saw below me that golden valley -
This land was made for you and me. *Chorus*

I roamed and rambled, and I followed my footsteps
To the sparkling sands of her diamond deserts,
And all around me a voice was sounding,
This land was made for you and me. *Chorus*

When the sun come shining, then I was strolling,
And the wheat fields waving, and the dust clouds rolling,
A voice was chanting as the fog was lifting.
This land was made for you and me. *Chorus*

To Come to America

In June 1991, I conducted a weeklong folksong workshop with third- and fourth-grade children at the Coman Hills School in Armonk, New York. The children came from many different ethnic backgrounds, and I asked them to discuss with their parents the reasons why their families came to America (in whatever generation that had occurred). The parents were glad to cooperate, and stimulated by these conversations, the children came up with reasons of their own as well as those they heard at home. We put a number of these thoughts into verse form and set them to the tune of the Irish immigrant song "Paddy Works on the Railway."

To Come to America

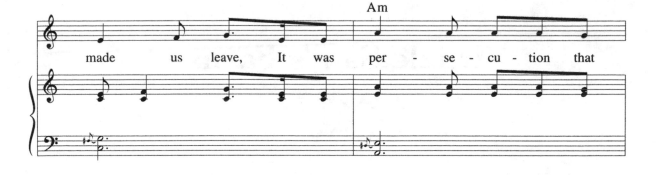

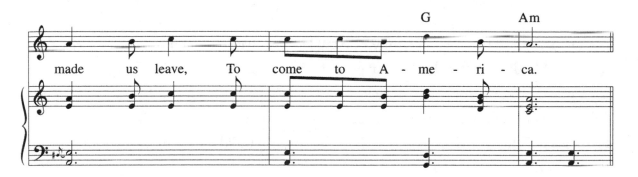

We didn't want to be pushed around,
We didn't want to be pushed around,
We didn't want to be pushed around,
   To come to America. *Chorus*

    Similarly

We wanted to get away from war…

We came to America to get good land…

I came to America to join my love…

We went from place to place to place…

We wanted to vote for a president…

We left out homes because we were poor…

It was Adolf Hitler that made us leave…

    And finally…

We wanted to have freedom there,
We wanted to have freedom there,
We wanted to have freedom there,
   So we came to America. *Chorus*

Uncle Sam's Farm

The singing Hutchinson family of New Hampshire was the most popular vocal ensemble during the thirty-year period preceding the Civil War. They are remembered chiefly for their antislavery and abolitionist songs. It was during this turbulent period that some 20 million people responded to America's "general invitation to the people of the world" to come to these shores and build a new life. The Hutchinsons wrote this song around 1850.

Uncle Sam's Farm

Words by Jesse Hutchinson

Music by the Hutchinson Family

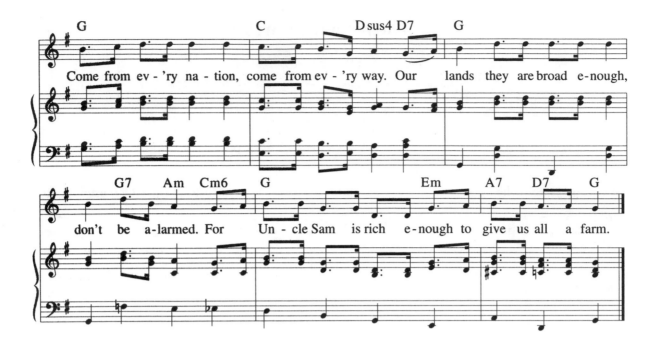

Come from ev-'ry na-tion, come from ev-'ry way. Our lands they are broad e-nough, don't be a-larmed. For Un-cle Sam is rich e-nough to give us all a farm.

St. Lawrence is our Northern line, far her waters flow,
And the Rio Grande our Southern bound, way down in Mexico;
While from the Atlantic Ocean where the sun begins to dawn,
We'll cross the Rocky Mountains far away to Oregon. *Chorus*

While the South shall raise the cotton, and the West the corn and pork,
New England manufactures shall do the finer work;
For the deep and flowing waterfalls that course along our hills,
Are just the thing for washing sheep and driving cotton mills. *Chorus*

Our fathers gave us liberty, but little did they dream
The grand results to follow in the mighty age of steam;
Our mountains, lakes and rivers are now in a blaze of fire,
While we send the news by lightning on the telegraphic wire. *Chorus*

While Europe's in commotion and her monarchs in a fret,
We're teaching them a lesson that they never can forget;
And this they fast are learning, Uncle Sam is not a fool,
For the people do their voting and the children go to school. *Chorus*

The brave in every nation are joining heart and hand,
And flocking to America, the real promised land;
And Uncle Sam stands ready with a child upon each arm,
To give them all a welcome to a lot upon his farm. *Chorus*

A welcome warm and hearty do we give the sons of toil,
To come to the West and settle and labor on Free Soil;
We've room enough and land enough, they needn't feel alarm -
Oh! Come to the land of Freedom and vote yourself a farm. *Chorus*

Yes, we're bound to lead the nations, for our motto's "Go Ahead!"
And we"ll carry out the principles for which our fathers bled;
No monopoly of kings and queens, but this is the Yankee plan:
Free Trade and Immigration, and Protection unto man. *Chorus*

We Shall Overcome

"We Shall Overcome" is an adaptation of the old Baptist hymn "I Shall Overcome." It was introduced in the late 1950s by members of the CIO Food and Tobacco Workers Union at the Highlander Folk School in Monteagle, Tennessee. During the Civil Rights Movement in the 1960s, it was picked up, brought up to date, and sung, first in the South, then all over the country, and finally all over the world. Over the years, the song has taken on added significance as a call for worldwide understanding, brotherhood, and peace.

We Shall Overcome

Musical and Lyrical Adaptation by Zilphia Horton, Frank Hamilton, Guy Carawan and Pete Seeger
Inspired by African American Gospel Singing, members of the Food and Tobacco Workers Union,
Charleston, SC. and the southern Civil Rights Movement
TRO - © Copyright 1960 (Renewed) and 1963 (Renewed) Ludlow Music, Inc. New York, NY
This arrangement TRO © Copyright 2001 Ludlow Music, Inc., New York, NY
International Copyright Secured   All Rights Reserved Including Public Performance For Profit
Royalties derived from this composition are being contributed to the We Shall Overcome Fund
and The Freedom Movement under the Trusteeship of the writers.

Americans All

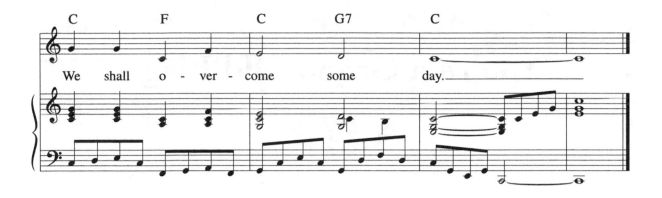

We'll walk hand in hand,
We'll walk hand in hand,
We'll walk hand in hand some day.
Oh, deep in my heart
I do believe,
We shall overcome some day.

Similarly

We shall live in peace…

We shall all be free…

We shall end Jim Crow…

We are not afraid…(today)

The Lord will see us through…

We are not alone…(today)

The whole wide world around…

We shall overcome…

You're a Grand Old Flag

When it comes to musical flag-waving, no composer has ever come close to George M. Cohan. Imagine Cohan's chagrin, then, when after the opening night of his show *George Washington, Jr.* on February 12, 1906, he was the subject of outraged attacks by patriotic organizations for having insulted the American flag! The reason? The original title of this song, "You're a Grand Old Rag," was deemed offensive by many. Fortunately, "flag" rhymes with "rag," and after a quick substitution of one for the other, all was forgiven, and the formerly offending song went on to become the hit number of the show.

"You're a Grand Old Flag" was performed by Cohan in the 1932 film *The Phantom President* and was featured in the 1942 film *Yankee Doodle Dandy.*

You're a Grand Old Flag

Words and Music by George M. Cohan

There's a feel-ing comes a - steal-ing and it sets my brain a - reel-ing When I'm list-'ning to the mu-sic of a mil - i - ta - ry band. An - y tune like "Yan-kee Doo-dle" sim-ply sets me off my noo-dle. It's that pa - tri - ot - ic some-thing that no

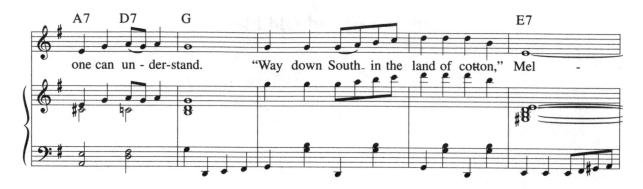

one can un-der-stand. "Way down South_ in the land of cotton," Mel -

o - dy un - tir - ing,_____ ain't that in - spi - ring?_____ Hur -

rah! Hur - rah! We'll join the ju - bi - lee. And that's go - ing

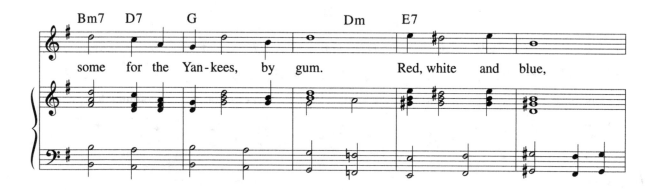

some for the Yan-kees, by gum. Red, white and blue,

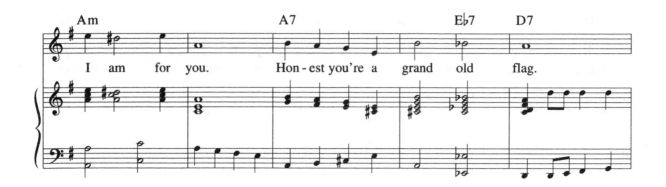

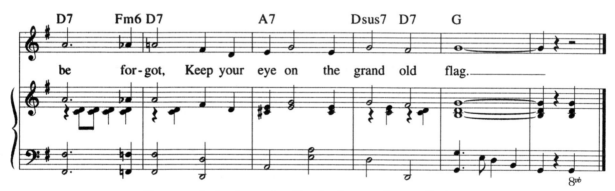

I'm a cranky hanky panky, I'm dead square honest Yankee,
And I'm mighty proud of that old flag that flies for Uncle Sam.
Though I don't believe in raving, ev'ry time I see it waving,
There's a chill runs up my back that makes me glad I'm what I am.
    Here's a land with a million soldiers;
    That's if we should need 'em, we'll fight for freedom.
    Hurrah! Hurrah! for ev'ry Yankee Tar and old G. A. R.
    Ev'ry stripe - ev'ry star.
    Red, white and blue, hats off to you;
    Honest, you're a grand old flag. *Chorus*

This Is My Country

The year 1940 was a good one for Tin Pan Alley. Sure, there was a war going on "over there," but America's songwriters weren't too concerned. At least, they didn't show it in their songs. America was boogying to "Beat Me Daddy, Eight to the Bar," swinging to "How High the Moon," crooning to "Sleepy Lagoon," and getting just a little sentimental to "The Last Time I Saw Paris." Irving Berlin, Hoagy Carmichael, Lorenz Hart, Richard Rogers, and Jerome Kern, to name but a few top songsmiths, all had big hits that year. Don Raye and Al Jacobs took a different route with their song "This Is My Country." A simple, hymnlike melody carrying unpretentious patriotic words, it stands apart from all the Broadway and Hollywood glitter and goes straight to our hearts. For this, after all, is *our* country.

This Is My Country

Words by Don Raye

Music by Al Jacobs

Americans All

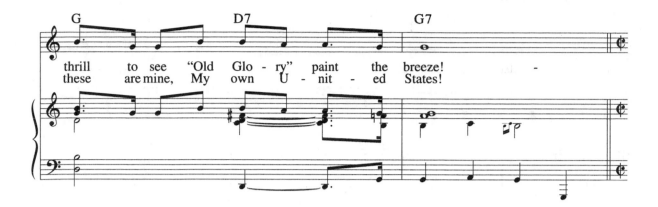

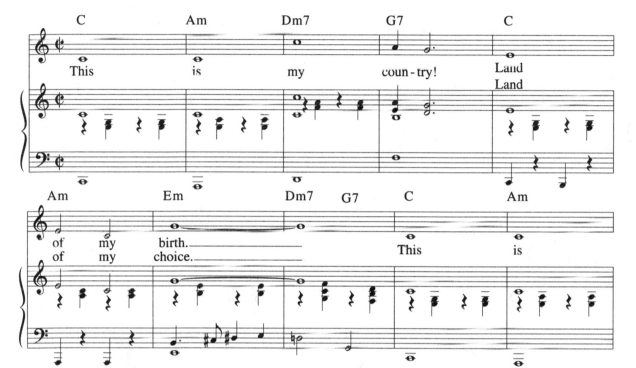

This Is My Country

I pledge thee my al-le-giance, A-me-ri-ca

the bold._____ For This is my

coun-try, to have and to hold!

hold!_____

The Yankee Doodle Boy

George M. Cohan missed being "born on the Fourth of July" by one day, coming into this world on July 3, 1878. Nevertheless, when his musical show *Little Johnny Jones* opened at the Liberty Theater in New York on November 7, 1904 (one day before Theodore Roosevelt was elected president), there was George onstage, playing the leading role and introducing the rousing "Yankee Doodle Boy" to universal acclaim. His mother, Helen, and father, Jerry, longtime headline vaudevillians in their own right, were in the show as well.

"The Yankee Doodle Boy" has endured over the years and was one of the featured numbers in the 1942 Academy Award–winning film *Yankee Doodle Dandy*, which starred James Cagney as song-and-dance man Cohan.

The Yankee Doodle Boy

Words and Music by George M. Cohan

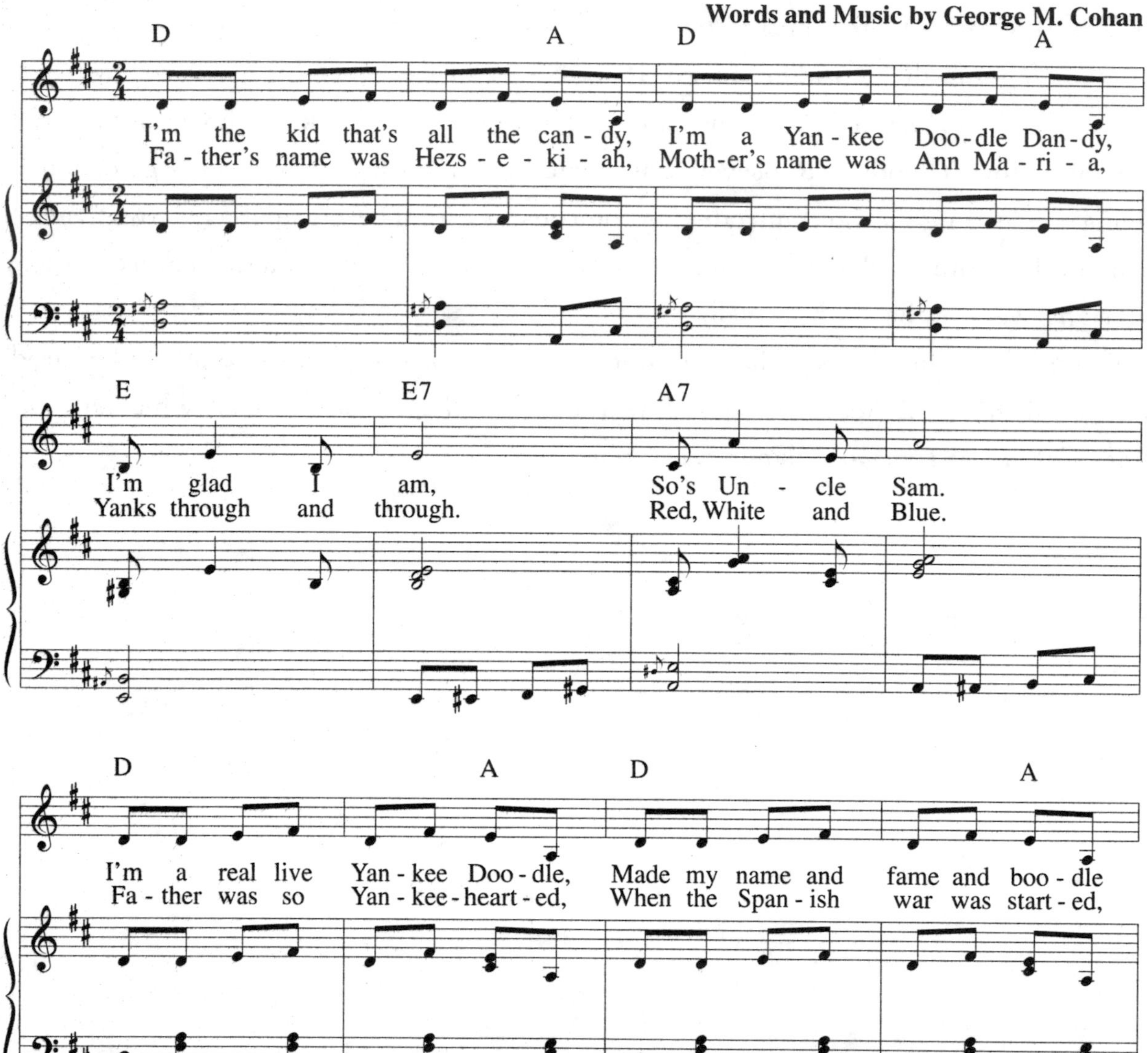

Just like Mis - ter Doo - dle did by rid - ing on a po - ny. I
He slipped on his u - ni - form and hopped up on a po - ny. My

love to lis - ten to the "Dix - ie" strain, "I long to see the girl I left be - hind me;" And
moth - er's moth - er was a Yan - kee true, My fa - ther's fa - ther was a Yan - kee, too: And

that ain't a josh, She's a Yan - kee, by gosh. Oh,
that's go - ing some, For the Yan - kees, by gum. Oh,

say can you see An - y -
say can you see An - y -

The Yankee Doodle Boy

thing a - bout a Yan - kee that's a pho - ny?
thing a - bout my pe - di - gree that's pho - ny?

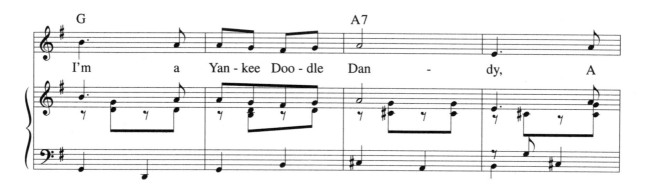

I'm a Yan - kee Doo - dle Dan - dy, A

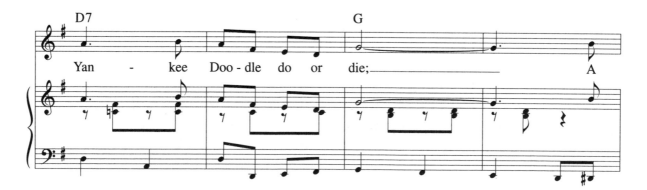

Yan - kee Doo - dle do or die;_____ A

The Yankee Doodle Boy

Yan - kee Doo - dle   came to Lon - don   Just to ride the   po — nies;

I   am   the   Yan - kee Doo - dle   Boy.